Gentile Folly: the Rothschilds

by

ARNOLD LEESE

Author of

"My Irrelevant Defence: Jewish Ritual Murder."

Both of these books obtainable from the Author, at
White House, Pewley Hill, Guildford.
Each book 1/- with postage for 4 ozs.

This book is dedicated, with permission, to
H. H. BEAMISH,
the pioneer, who set my feet upon the way.

"If I am killing a rat with a stick and have him in a corner,
I am not indignant if he tries to bite me and squeals and
gibbers with rage. My job is, not to get angry, but to keep
cool, to attend to my footwork and to keep on hitting him
where it will do the most good."—

A. S. Leese, speaking at Reception, 17th Feb., 1937, on his
return from prison where he was consigned for writing the
truth about Jews.

ISBN: 978-2-925369-80-6
Printed in the USA.

CONTENTS

PREFACE.

THIS little book has been produced with the object of filling a vacancy which the author considers has too long existed. Works on the Rothschilds are many, but nearly all these are either purposefully inaccurate or, like Count Corti's masterpiece, long and rather dry. This book of mine contains no padding and needs to be read slowly.

I am not concerned with anecdotes about the Rothschilds, nor with registering their "wise-cracks," nor with their "charity." I take no interest in the Rothschilds as men or robots, but only as Jews; this book, which has been condensed so as to be within the reach of any working-man or woman, deals with the principal aspects of *control over the Gentile* by sheer weight of money-power, a control used for purposes *not* Gentile.

Dealing, as it does, with the last 150 years which have been so full of world-shaking events, it has been no easy task to squeeze what I have to say within the compass of a one-shilling publication. To enable those who have either forgotten their history or (let us be honest) never learned it, to follow the narrative more easily, a calendar of some of the principal historical events of the period follows this preface, and I would advise the reader to have within reach, when reading the book, an ordinary school history-book for occasional reference.

On the page following the Calendar, the reader will find a list of the principal works from which quotations, etc., have been taken, together with the letters of the alphabet used as references to them. Thus, for example, the sign (B, Vol. IV. p. 272) refers to that volume and page in the *Jewish Encyclopædia*.

In attempting my task, I know that I am only able to expose a small fraction of the total evil done by certain members of this Jewish family in the past; but, like a geologist who tells the story of the earth by his observations upon outcrops of rock, I tell the story of Rothschild control over the Gentiles from the evidence which has happened to come to light, so that my readers may judge for themselves what still lies underground.

Trusting that this book may enable others to dispense knowledge of the subject, I now drop this spanner into the wobbling, squeaking, overheated machinery of an outworn democracy, hoping for the best. I ask my readers to get busy, for the time is short.

ARNOLD LEESE.

White House,
Pewley Hill,
Guildford.

28th February, 1940.

A FEW HISTORICAL LANDMARKS
FOR THE READER'S GUIDANCE.

1789. French Revolution.
1793. Louis XVI. beheaded.
1804. Bonaparte made Emperor Napoleon 1st.
1806. Napoleon shattered Prussia at Battle of Jena.
1808-13. Peninsular War.
1812. Napoleon's Retreat from Moscow.
        Napoleon defeated at Leipzig and abdicated, being exiled to Elba.
1814-15 Vienna Congress to settle the affairs of Europe.
1815. Napoleon returns, the "hundred days," Battle of Waterloo.
        Return of Bourbon Kings.
1830 Second French Revolution. Charles X. expelled. Louis Phillippe,
        Duke of Orleans, became King of France.
1836. Don Carlos claimed Spanish throne; war ended in his defeat.
1848. Third French Revolution, Louis Philippe dethroned; Republic
        proclaimed. Similar disturbances in other European States.
1851. Louis Napoleon voted President of French Republic.
1852. Louis Napoleon becomes Emperor as Napoleon III.
1854-6. Crimean War.
1860. Italy united by Garibaldi.
1861. Civil War in America between North and South over Slavery.
        It continued until 1865.
1864. Outbreak of Seven Years' War between Prussia and Austria.
1870. Franco-Prussian War. Napoleon III. abdicated, and France
        became Republic,
1871. Communist insurrection in Paris. On restoration of order, Thiers
        elected President of French Republic.
1877. Russo-Turkish War.
1878. Treaty of Berlin, settling affairs of Turkey.
1881. Death of Disraeli (Lord Beaconsfield), principal Rothschild
        agent in England.
        Transvaal wins self-government under British suzerainty.
1888. De Beers Diamond monopoly formed.
1895. Jameson Raid.
1899-1902. Boer War ending in defeat of President Kruger.
1901. Death of Queen Victoria.
1910. Death of King Edward VII.
1914-18. Great World War, followed by Versailles Conference.
1915. Sir H. McMahon promises Palestine to the Arabs.
1917. "Liberal" Revolution in Russia quickly followed by Bolshevik
        revolution.
        Lord Balfour promises Palestine to the Jews.
1939. Beginning of the Jewish War of revenge against Hitler.

Works frequently referred to in the Text.

A. *The Rise and the Reign of the House of Rothschild*, by Count Corti, in 2 volumes, 1928. This is a work of independent historical research of great value, completely documented, but naturally a little long and dry for ordinary readers.

B *Jewish Encyclopædia*, Vols. 1 to XII. Published between 1903 and 1906, an authoritative reference book by Jews, representing their own interpretation of Jewish and other activities.

C. *The Riddle of the Jews' Success*, by F. Roderick-Stoltheim, translated by C. Pownall. Hammer Verlag publication, 1927.

D. *Letters and Friendships of Sir Cecil Spring Rice*, 2 vols., 1929. Edited by S. Gwynn.

E. *L'Anti-semitisme*, by the Jew Bernard Lazare, 1894.

F. *Occult Theocrasy*, by Lady Queenborough, published posthumously, for private circulation only, 2 vols.

G. *Life and Memoirs of Count Mole*, edited by Marquis of Noailles, 2 vols., 1923.

H. *Essays in Jewish History*, by the Jew L. Wolf, 1934.

J. *The Financiers and the Nation*, by T. Johnston, 1934.

K. *Greville Diary*, edited by P. W. Wilson, 1927. Chas. Greville was Clerk to the Privy Council for many years. The references given are the dates of the entries cited.

L. *The Magnificent Rothschilds*, by the Jew C. Roth, 1939.

M. *Lady Rothschild and her Daughters*, by L. Cohen, 1935.

N. *The Life of Lord Beaconsfield*, by T. P. O'Connor, M.P.

O. *Aus meinem Leben und aus meiner Zeit*, by Duke Ernst II of Saxe-Coburg-Gotha, Berlin, 1888, 2 Vols.

P. *Diary of Lord Bertie*, 1914-18, edited by Lady Algernon G. Lennox, 1924. Lord Bertie was our Paris Ambassador, 1905-18.

Q. *World Hoax*, by E. F. Elmhurst, 1938, U S.A.

R. *Encyclopædia Britannica*, 11th edition.

S. *The Life of Lord George Bentinck*, by the Jew Disraeli. There are many editions of this book, so all references are to Chapters.

T. *History of the Jews in Vienna*, by the Jew M. Grunwald, 1936, Jewish Publication Society of America.

Works frequently referred to in the Text.—Continued.

U. *My Irrelevant Defence; Jewish Ritual Murder*, by A. S. Leese, 1937.

V. *Grey Wolf*, by H. C. Armstrong, a study of Mustafa Kemal.

W. *Reminiscences*, by the Jewess Lady Battersea, 1922. She was a Rothschild.

X. *Letters of Charles Greville and Henry Reeve*, edited by A. H. Johnson, 1924.

Y. *My Autobiography*, by Margot Asquith.

Z. *Merchants of Death*, by H. C. Engelbrecht and F. C. Hanighen, 1934. ·

Z.1 *The Oil War*, by A. Mohr, 1926.

Z.2 *The Secret War for Oil*, by F. C. Hanighen and A. Zischka, 1935. This book was published by Geo. Routledge & Sons but withdrawn from circulation about one week later.

Z.3 *Fifty Years in Wall Street*, by H. Clews, 1908, Irving Publishing Co., New York. Clews was himself a Wall Street man, genuinely ignorant of the Jew menace.

Z.4 *Dictionary of American Biography*, edited by A. Johnson, 1929. In many volumes.

Z.5 *Money Powers of Europe in the 19th and 20th Century*, by the Jew Paul H. Emden, 1939.

A COMPANION VOLUME TO THIS WORK IS
" *My Irrelevant Defence : Jewish Ritual Murder.*"
By A. S. LEESE.

Price One Shilling, plus postage—1d. open, 2d. closed.

Obtainable only from the author,

White House, Pewley Hill, Guildford.

A ROTHSCHILD STUD-BOOK

1st Generation :—

Mayer Amschel, 1744-1812. He had 5 sons and 5 daughters.

2nd and 3rd Generations :—

These are the 5 sons of Amschel Mayer and their children.

1. Amschel Mayer, Frankfort, 1773-1885. He had no children.
2. Solomon, Vienna, 1774-1885, had 1 son and 1 daughter. The son was Anselm Solomon, 1803-74.
3. Nathan Mayer, London, 1777-1836, had 4 sons and 3 daughters. The 4 sons were :—
   Lionel Nathan, 1808-79.
   Anthony, 1810-76, Baronet.
   Nathaniel, 1812-70.
   Mayer Amschel, 1818-1874.
4. Karl Mayer, Naples, 1788-1855, had 3 sons and 2 daughters. The 3 sons were :—
   Mayer Karl, 1820-86.
   Wilhelm Karl, 1828-1901.
   Adolf, 1823-1900. He had no children.
5. James, Paris, 1792-1868. He had 4 sons and 1 daughter. The 4 sons were :—
   Alphonse, 1827-1905.
   Solomon, 1835-64.
   Gustav, 1829.
   Edmond, 1845-1917.

4th Generation :—

Anselm, had 3 sons and 4 daughters. The sons were :—
   Ferdinand, 1839-1898. He had no children.
   Nathaniel, 1830-1905. Ditto.
   Albert Solomon, 1844-1911.
Lionel Nathan, had 3 sons and 2 daughters. The sons were :—
   Nathaniel, 1840-1915 (1st " English " Baron).
   Alfred, 1842-1918. Had no legitimate children.
   Leopold, 1845-1917.
Anthony, Sir, Bart., had 2 daughters.
Nathaniel, had 3 sons and 1 daughter. The sons were :—
   Jas. Edward, 1844-84.
   Albert, 1846-50.
   Arthur, 1851-1903.
Mayer Amschel (son of Nathan Mayer) had a daughter, Hannah.
Mayer Karl, had 7 daughters, no sons.
Wilhelm Karl, had 2 daughters, no sons.
Alphonse, had 1 son and 2 daughters. The son was :—
   Edouard Alphonse Jas., b. 1868.
Solomon (son of Jas.), had 1 daughter.
Gustav, had 2 sons and 3 daughters. The sons were :—
   Andre, b. 1874.
   Robert Philippe, b. 1880.
Edmond, had 2 sons and 1 daughter. The sons were :—
   Jas. Edmond, b. 1878.
   Maurice Edmond, b. 1881.

5th Generation :—

Albert Solomon (son of Anselm), had 3 sons and 1 daughter. The sons were :—

George, b. 1877, died, no children.

Alfons, b. 1878.

Louis, b. 1882.

Eugene, b. 1884.

Nathaniel (son of Lionel Nathan), had 2 sons and 1 daughter. The sons were :—

Lionel Walter, 2nd "English" Baron, 1868-1937. Did not marry.

Nathaniel Chas., 1877-1923.

Leopold, had 2 sons and 1 daughter. The sons were :—

Lionel Nathan, b. 1882.

Anthony Gustav, b. 1887.

Jas. Edward (son of Nathaniel), had a son and a daughter. The son was :—

Henri, b. 1872.

Edouard Alphonse (son of Alphonse), had a son :—

Guy, b. 1909.

6th Generation :—

Alfons (son of Albert), had 1 son and 2 daughters. The son was :—
Albert, b. 1922.

Nathaniel Chas. (son of Nathaniel, and grandson of Lionel Nathan), had a son and 3 daughters. The son was :—

Nathaniel Mayer Victor, 3rd "English" Baron, b. 1913.

Lionel Nathan (son of Leopold), had 2 sons and 2 daughters. The sons were :—

Edmund Leopold, b. 1916.

Leopold David, b. 1927.

Anthony Gustav, had 1 son and 2 daughters. The son was :—
Evelyn Robert, b. 1931.

Henri, had 2 sons and 1 daughter. The sons were :—

Jas. Nathaniel, b. 1896.

Philippe, b. 1902.

7th Generation :—

Nathaniel Mayer Victor Rothschild has a son, Nathaniel Charles Jacob, b. 1936.

NOTE.

Among the earlier Rothschilds (that is, the three generations following the founder of the House, Amschel Mayer), marriage was generally a business affair, and it was a common practice for males to marry other Rothschilds and for superfluous females to marry where more business might be expected as a result. And so we get this staggering fact from the *Jewish Encyclopædia* (B, Vol. X, p. 497) : "Of 58 marriages contracted by the descendants of Mayer Amschel Rothschild, to date (1905) no less than 29, or exactly one-half, have been between first cousins."

Betty Rothschild, daughter of Solomon, actually married her uncle, Baron James of Paris, whilst Anselm Rothschild married his niece, the daughter of Nathaniel.

GENTILE FOLLY: THE ROTHSCHILDS

THE founder of the Rothschild financial power was Mayer Amschel Rothschild (1743-1812), born in the Frankfort ghetto; his father was a banker and sent his son to study for the rabbinate, but the latter was more attracted by the handling of money, and took a post in Oppenheim's bank at Hanover. In 1760, he started business for himself at Frankfort when only 17 years of age. It is interesting to note that the house in which he lived, which was divided into two parts, was owned, until Amschel purchased it, by the forebears of Jacob Schiff, the Jew who became head of the New York firm of Jew bankers Kuhn Loeb & Co. In fact, Jacob Schiff's father was broker to the Rothschilds.

At that period, the Landgrave of Hesse-Cassel, Frederick II., was one of the richest men in Europe, having made immense sums by hiring out his subjects as mercenaries to serve in the armies of other nations, particularly Britain. These mercenaries were the "Hessian troops" we heard so much about at school. But as Amschel Rothschild never contacted Frederick II. in business matters, he had nothing to do with the arrangements made for the hiring of the Hessians, drunken and useless as they were, to attempt to subdue the Americans in their revolt known as the War of Independence, 1773-83. It is necessary to emphasise this, as the contrary is often stated in anti-Jewish books. It was the firm of Van der Notten in England that handled the financing of that business. But Frederick's son and heir, William, took an interest in coin-collecting, which Amschel Rothschild cunningly served and so gradually obtained some sort of notice from William. This was the beginning of the association of the Rothschilds with the house of Hesse-Cassel which laid the foundation of the Rothschild Money Power. Worming his way into William's favour by means of supplying him with rare coins for the latter's collection, Amschel began to gain William's interest, although not yet his confidence.

In 1769, when he was only 25 years old, Amschel secured from William the designation of Crown Agent to Hesse-Hanau, but this was a mere title without official status, so Amschel found it necessary to cultivate the favour of William's treasurer Buderus to assist him gradually to overcome the suspicion with which William naturally regarded him. Apart from bill-discounting for William who had succeeded his father as Landgrave of Hesse-Cassel in 1785, a business which had to be shared with many others, no big business for William came into Rothschild's hands until 1800. William of Hesse-Cassel was now enormously rich by inheritance.

But Amschel had many other irons in the fire, connected with financing and trading in the war-necessities of the countries engaged in the struggle with Napoleon, and by 1800, he was, chiefly through such work, the tenth richest Jew in Frankfort. By this time he had worked himself into the Landgrave's favour, and in 1803 (during which year William was promoted to the title and powers of Elector) Rothschild acted as middleman in secret for the loan of the Elector's money to Denmark, and from that time frequently invested large sums for William with handsome commissions and perquisites. Rothschild had a large family to support, of which his five sons were Amschel (whom I shall call Amschel II.), Solomon, Nathan, Karl and James. As is well-known, these five sons ultimately managed branches of the Rothschild business in the principal financial centres of Europe, Amschel II. succeeding his father in Frankfort, Solomon settling in Vienna, Nathan in London, Karl in Naples and James in Paris. At the period with which we are now dealing, the only son to leave the Frankfort ghetto was the most cunning of them all, Nathan, who came to England where he did some very sharp practice connected with monopolising raw material for Manchester's manufactures, and this when he was only 21 years old. After that, in 1804, he set up business in London and we shall follow his fortunes in Chapter II.

In 1806, Napoleon shattered the Prussians at Jena, and Elector William had to seek safety in flight, leaving his business affairs and treasures to his trusted agents : there is a romantic tale, which must now be " de-bunked," that before leaving he entrusted everything to Amschel Rothschild ; a Jew artist of Frankfort, Moritz Oppenheim, has endeavoured to perpetuate the romance by painting a picture showing the Elector patting Amschel on the shoulder whilst lackeys carry boxes of specie into the latter's house. Actually, the Rothschilds were only entrusted with four boxes of securities and papers, the bulk of the Elector's treasure being distributed for hiding elsewhere (A, Vol. I, p. 66). Buderus, the Elector's treasurer, was still unable to imbue his master with much faith in Rothschild, although eventually the latter was able to give full satisfaction to his exalted client when William returned to Hesse-Cassel in 1812 after Napoleon's defeat at Leipzic. Rothschild's success in farming the Elector's credit under the accommodating eye of Buderus was due to the fact that he was favouring both sides, for he had also wormed his way into the high favour of Napoleon's representative, Carl von Dalberg, who had been made Prince-Primate of the Confederation of the Rhine and later Grand Duke of Frankfort. " There would appear to have been financial reasons for this relationship, and it no doubt originated in loans granted by Rothschild " (A, Vol. I., p. 69). For example, one such loan was made to Dalberg by Amschel in 1811 to enable him to travel to Paris on the occasion of the baptism of the son of Napoleon and Marie Louise. No wonder, then, that the *Jewish Encyclopedia* (B, Vol. IV., p. 413) records that Dalberg favoured the complete emancipation of

the Jews and actually obtained it for them in return for a cash consideration of 440,000 florins !

Rothschild did not rely merely upon the favour of one of Napoleon's
men ; he was also very friendly with Dalberg's Police Commissioner, a
Jew called von Itzstein.

In 1810, Rothschild was powerful enough to make a huge loan of
his own money to Denmark.

In 1812, Amschel Rothschild died. It is to be noted that only two
of his five sons at this time were settled abroad, namely, Nathan in
England, and James who had gone in 1811 to Paris where we shall
meet him again in Chapter III. Amschel II. took over his father's
office at Frankfort. He sent his brother Solomon to open offices in
Vienna in 1816, and his brother Karl to Naples in 1821. He nego-
tiated immense loans to Austria, Prussia and to France (under
Louis XVIII.) and secured for himself and all his brothers titles of
Austrian nobility, a development culminating in 1822 in them all
becoming Barons of the Austrian Empire. The only brother who did
not assume the title was Nathan in England.

It was late in Amschel II.'s life when he became acquainted with
Bismarck. In 1851 Amschel II persistently curried Bismarck's favour
when the latter came to Frankfort as Prussia's representative. At first
these servile overtures were regarded by Bismarck with some amuse-
ment, but nevertheless we find him in the same year accepting the use
of a residence from Rothschild (A, Vol. II., p. 317) and in 1853 the
Rothschilds became Court Bankers to Prussia. From about 1852, the
Rothschilds were high in Bismarck's favour.

This registers the usual change of view by Gentile politicians
coming under the pernicious influence of Jewish favours and money
power. In 1847 Bismarck had declared he was not in favour of allowing Jews to occupy official positions in a Christian State, the function
of which was the realisation of Christian teaching. Yet in 1869 it was
under his Chancellorship that Jews were completely emancipated. How
much this was due to the Rothschilds and how much to other Jews'
influence, can only be guessed. Bismarck's most familiar Jew was
Baron Gerson von Bleichroder who founded a banking syndicate with
the Rothschilds after 1866 and represented that firm in Berlin and
Prussia generally.

Amschel II. died in 1855, and the Rothschild firm in Frankfort was
taken over by Mayer Karl Rothschild, his nephew, son of Karl of
Naples, assisted by his brother William. The latter took over on
Mayer Carl's death in 1886 but under him the firm did not prosper and
closed in 1901 on William's decease, the Disconto Gesellschaft taking
over the local connection.

In the years between, Bleichroder in Berlin and Alphonse Rothschild
(James's son) in Paris were the secret purveyors of news to Bismarck
and Napoleon III, being in constant communication. They were thus
able to tell Bismarck what they thought he ought to know about
Napoleon III., and Napoleon what they thought he ought to know
about Bismarck. During the Franco-Prussian War it was in Alphonse

Rothschild's castle at Ferrieres that Bismarck made his headquarters when besieging Paris. The same two Jews, Bleichroder for Prussia and Alphonse Rothschild for France, made the arrangements for the satisfactory payment of the indemnity by the vanquished, which reminds one of the similar situation at Versailles after the Great War when the Jewish bankers Warburg had a member of the family as financial adviser on each side, one for America, one for Germany.

A curious occurence took place at a protest meeting against Hitler's treatment of the Jews, at the Pavilion Theatre, Whitechapel Road, on 10th December, 1934. An excited Jew speaker, M. Soman, claimed Bismarck as a Jew.

That Bismarck might have had some Jewish blood is not such an absurd proposition after all. Frightened Jews sometimes blurt out the unaccustomed truth. Bismarck's mother was born a Mencken, a common Jewish name, whilst there is some doubt as to Bismarck's actual paternity, one author, not remarkable for his general accuracy, believing that Marshal Soult was his real father, Soult being identified as a Jew by Disraeli in *Coningsby*. Certainly, Bismarck's son Herbert had none of the healthy Aryan's repugnance to Jews as he actually proposed to the half-Jewish daughter of Duke Ludwig of Bavaria (*My Past*, by Countess Larisch, Chapter II.)

C. Spring Rice in a letter written when he was Second Secretary to our Embassy at Berlin in 1897 said that Rothschild's agent was admitted into the German Foreign Office before the Ambassadors of the Powers (D, letter dated 7th November, 1897). The press, he also said, was almost entirely in Jewish hands.

In 1878, the Jew banker Max von Goldschmidt of Frankfort married William Rothschild's daughter and changed his name to Goldschmidt-Rothschild.

* * * * * *

During the period of Europe's history in which the first Amschel Rothschild was established at Frankfort, the French Revolution stands out as by far the most important political event; it is now established that it came about under the influence of Freemasonry and the subversive society behind Masonry, known as the Illuminati. Seeing that the Jews obtained emancipation in France only two years after the Revolution, and that the new social order imposed by the Revolution summed up in the catch-cry "Liberty, Equality, Fraternity" was based upon false destructive principles typically Jewish, it is necessary to see what relationship the Rothschilds of the period may have had with regard to the outbreak.

Illuminism penetrated into all the Lodges of Grand Orient Freemasonry in France, being backed by organised cabbalistic Jews. (E.) According to F, Vol. I., p. 184, the Jewish financiers behind the 1789 Revolution were as follows (their dates, places of abode and some other details have been added) :—

Daniel Itzig, 1722-1799, Berlin, Court Jew to Frederick William II.

David Friedlander, 1750-1834, Berlin, his son-in-law.

Herz Cerfbeer, 1730-1793, Alsace.

Benjamin Goldsmid, 1755-1808, London, William Pitt's (the younger) financier.

Abraham Goldsmid, 1756-1810, London, his brother.

Moses Mocatta, 1768-1857, London, partner of a brother of the two Goldsmids, and uncle of Sir Moses Montefiore.

Lady Queenborough's list also includes V. H. Ephraim, Court Jew to Frederick William I., and to Frederick the Great ; but his work was preparatory to the Revolution, and he died 14 years before it came about.

There is absolutely no evidence that I have found to connect the first Amschel Rothschild directly with the 1789 Revolution. He most emphatically was *not* the *alter ego* of Frederick, Landgrave of Hesse-Cassel, as has been stated by a certain author, and never had anything to do with that potentate, at whose palace in Wilhelmsbad the notorious Masonic Congress was held in which Illuminism definitely allied itself to Freemasonry, the Landgrave himself being Grand Master of Bavarian Masonry. This was in 1782, and the headquarters of Illuminised Masonry was set up in Frankfort in the same year. But at that time, Amschel Rothschild had no considerable influence even with Frederick's son, and none at all with the Landgrave himself.

There was, however, an organisation formed at Berlin called the League of Virtue or *Tugenbuud*, which was, in the words of the Special Commissioner of Police at Mayence " so identified with the Illuminati that no line of demarcation was seen between them " (1814, Archives Nationales F 7/6563). The headquarters of the Tugenbund were at the house of a Jewish member of the Illuminati, Herz, friend and pupil of Moses Mendelssohn, the Jewish "intellectual" revolutionary ; Herz's wife, Henrietta, usually presided at the gatherings. Among its adherents were two of Mendelssohn's daughters, who had two brothers married to members of the family of the Jew Daniel Itzig ; Mirabeau, who according to Graetz's *History of the Jews*, Vol. V., was more often in Mrs. Herz's company than her husband, and who introduced Illuminism into France and initiated the Duke of Orleans and Talleyrand into the order (F, Vol. I., p. 374) ; Fanny von Arnstein, daughter of Daniel Itzig, who ran a similar salon in Vienna ; William von Humboldt, who later became Prussian Ambassador in London, and his brother, the explorer Alexander von Humboldt who learned Hebrew from Mrs. Herz. But the most prominent member of the Tugenbund was Frederick von Gentz, a crypto-Jew " intellectual " quite unburdened by any morals, who later became secretary to Prince Metternich, Chancellor of Austria.

We have it on the authority of the *Jewish Chronicle*, 1st Sept., 1922, that Mrs. Herz herself said that the Tugenbund Jews were ardent supporters of the French Revolution.

Now, although Amschel the first cannot be incriminated as supporting the Illuminati, it is a striking fact that members of his family had the closest relations with some of the above-mentioned members of the Tugenbund.

It was von Gentz to whom the Rothschilds owed their later position with Prince Metternich of Austria (A, Vol. II., p. 69), although the first meeting between one of Amschel's sons and von Gentz did not take place until 1818. It is noteworthy that William von Humboldt's estates were managed by Amschel Rothschild II. in 1830, whilst as early as 1818 Alexander von Humboldt was, with his brother, in intimate social relationship with Nathan Rothschild in London (A, Vol. I., p. 215). It is simply impossible to believe that the five Rothschild sons were not secretly supporting the Revolutionary cause in France through the first half of the nineteenth century.

Fortunately, however, we have a decisive piece of evidence which puts the matter beyond dispute. It will be noted that Solomon Rothschild was not sent permanently to Vienna until 1816, when he was 42 years of age. Before that, he was assisting his father at Frankfort. Here, at a date not known but previous to 1814 and probably in his father's lifetime, although that is uncertain, he became a member of a Grand Orient Lodge of Freemasons called *L'Aurore Naissante*; this is shown in a report of the Director of Police at Graetz. (Reference *Les Dessous du Congres de Vienna*, by Commandant M. H. Weil, published by Libraire Payot in 1917, which, in turn obtained its data from original documents of the Ministry of Interior, Vienna, the reference being p.p. 419 and 420, Vienna, 6th Nov., 1814, F, 34468 and 3565). This Lodge was later taken over by the United Grand Lodge of England, a curious fact, but one which does not concern us here, since the transfer did not take place until 1817 (*History of Freemasonry*, by R. F. Gould, Vol. III., p.p. 236/7).

It is also to be noted that the Montefiore family, which is so closely intermarried with the Rothschilds, is also connected by marriage with the Goldsmids whose forebears Benjamin and Abraham are mentioned above as Jew financiers of the French Revolution, and that the sister of another of these, Moses Mocatta, was mother of Sir Moses Montefiore who became jackal to the London Rothschild House.

In 1807, another Tugenbund was formed, apparently with the genuine political object of uniting Germany against Napoleon; Amschel Rothschild had very close relations with it and " the Rothschilds appear to have become members " (A, Vol. I., p. 81). William of Hesse-Cassel was an important member and the Rothschilds acted as go-betweens for his correspondence concerning it and made payments in favour of the Tugenbund.

CHAPTER II

THE LONDON HOUSE.

WE left Nathan Mayer Rothschild in London, after his business adventures in Manchester. He started the London office in 1804, and was naturalised as an Englishman in two years! Working in conjunction with his father at Frankfort, he was able to handle huge sums on the Elector of Hesse-Cassel's account, moneys which he was commissioned to invest in British funds. The Peninsular War offered him unrivalled opportunities of profit. One of his earlier transactions was to purchase gold from the East India Company; this he was able to do by the use of the Elector's money at his disposal; then he sold the gold to the Government at a large profit and undertook the transmission of it to the battlefields in Spain. He had had previous experience of this sort of thing, because he had for some time been buying Wellington's paper cheaply, cashing it at the Treasury and sending the cash to Spain through France, the enemy's territory! All this was made possible by the fact that his brothers James, Karl and Solomon were at that time free to work in France; these brothers smuggled the cash through as far as Paris, where it was paid into banks, which provided the Rothschilds with bills on Spanish and other banks, which bills were in turn smuggled through to Wellington in Spain. We shall see, when we come to consider the activities of James Rothschild at Paris how all this could be done right under the nose of Napoleon. France was being made the vehicle through which Wellington was financing his campaign against Napoleon!

Both before and after Waterloo, England made heavy loans to her allies on the Continent, and Nathan soon got the lion's share in this work owing to his family's business connections.

Somewhere about 1806, Napoleon began to become Jew-wise. Previous to that date, the Jews had used him as a convenient and efficient tool for strengthening the revolutionary forces. It was in 1806 that he called together an assembly of representative Jews and offered them protection if they would abandon their scandalous commercial practices, particularly usury; it is obvious that Napoleon was seeking the best solution for everyone concerned in France; he was a firm believer in the literal truth of Genesis (G, p. 139), but "I cannot regard as Frenchmen," he said, "these Jews who suck the blood of true Frenchmen." In a letter to his brother Jerome, dated 6th March, 1808, he wrote —"I do not want any more of them (Jews) in my kingdom. Indeed I have done everything to prove my scorn of the most vile nation in the world."

Napoleon had realised also the true nature of money, and knew that the real credit of France was derived from the work of French people and not from stores of bullion owned by Jews.

From this time therefore, the full force of Jewry and of its ally Masonry was brought to bear on him to secure his defeat. There is good reason to suppose that the · Jews' share in bringing about

Napoleon's downfall amounted to much more than mere money-lending to his enemies. Disraeli in his novel *Coningsby* revealed that Marshal Soult was a Jew, and he is not likely to have made a mistake over such a matter, although the *Jewish Encyclopedia* denies the truth of the statement. Anyhow, Napoleon complained bitterly of the way Soult failed him at the Battle of Waterloo.

Nathan Rothschild made a tremendous profit by getting early news of the defeat of Napoleon at Waterloo, and buying up depressed stocks in an anxious England before the man-in-the-street was aware of Wellington's and Blucher's success. He shared his knowledge with the Government, no doubt, because to have done otherwise would obviously have deprived him of the Government's confidence and prevented future business dealings.

A romantic story has been published over and over again to the effect that Nathan himself was at Waterloo watching the battle, and that when the result was apparent, he galloped to the coast on swift horses, crossed the stormy sea at great danger to his life, and did some more galloping to London so as to get in first with the news to profit on it. This, of course, is rubbish; it takes a man in hard condition to do that galloping act, which would be impossible for a Jew of Nathan's wretched type; whilst the idea of a Rothschild of that generation risking himself in a stormy sea is too absurd for credence. Actually the prosaic fact is that Rothschild had an agent at Dunkirk, who, probably by means of cash advanced for the purpose, secured the first newspaper account in the Brussels *Gazette* hot from the press, risked the passage over a rough sea, and reported to Nathan who never left London.

The Rothschilds were not by any means universally trusted, but when they failed to obtain the handling of a loan, they resorted to the operation known as " bearing." They would employ every means of propaganda to attack and depress the stocks of governments which had employed other agents for raising the loans. After a few experiences of this sort, many governments who did not wish to employ the Rothschilds had to surrender and give them a share in the work for fear of the possible consequences if they did not do so.

" Prohibit ' bear ' sales " says honest Chas. W. Smith in his *Economic Ruin of the World* " and all power is taken out of the hands of cunning unscrupulous intriguers and market manipulators .... Do away with ' fictitious ' dealings, and no ten Rothschilds, Rockefellers or Pierpont Morgans combined could corner or smash any of the world's leading commodities or shares."

For the purpose of giving and receiving early news Nathan Rothschild established his own courier service, whilst he made full use of bribery of officials to obtain confidential information. He also had a carrier-pigeon service. Sometimes if it paid him to do so, he would share this early information, and it was Talleyrand who wrote that the English Cabinet always obtained information from Rothschild ten or twelve hours before the arrival of the official despatches (H, p. 273).

" Nathan issued the public loans of his period, always unloading them of course on the public at a higher price than he paid for them to the British Treasury. When he had sold the stock, he was not content, but must needs juggle with the market, depressing it with false rumours, then purchasing back the stock; and then again disseminating good news and elevating the market, he would sell the stock once more and reap another profit." (J, p. 12).

From 1824 to 1829 the Rothschilds loaned huge sums to Brazil; "Brazil, since 1825 might have been described as a Rothschild State." (J, p. 9).

In 1824, Nathan founded the Alliance Assurance Company in opposition to the Gentile companies, particularly Lloyd's. Sir Moses Montefiore was his Jew partner in the venture. Now, after 100 years we find both the companies, Alliance and Lloyd's, united in one racket. (See p. 25).

In 1830, a proposal was made by the Government to the East India Company for the reduction of its dividends; the Rothschilds, who had £40,000 of East India stock, sold it all out. Undoubtedly it was Rt. Hon. J. C. Herries, then in the Cabinet as Master of the Mint and President of the Board of Trade, who gave the Rothschilds notice of the intended change. (K, letter 9th Jan., 1830). Herries had always been hand-in-glove with Nathan ever since he had been comptroller of accounts in the Napoleonic Wars. (It is significant that Herries' son was made Chairman of the Board of Revenue by Disraeli in 1877).

Nathan's last big operation was that of raising a loan of 20 million pounds to compensate slave-owners in 1833 for the loss of their slaves.

Nathan died in 1836; in his will, he left his three daughters £100,000 a-piece provided they only married with their mother's and brothers' consent; otherwise, they got nothing. Marriage with the Rothschilds was just a matter of business. He bequeathed nothing to charity or to servants and dependants.

He had four sons, and of these it was Lionel who took the leadership of the business.

*   *   *   *   *   *

Lionel had the easy job of using the money power that his father had left in his hands as a political weapon. It was the Jews' interest and object to make Britain strong and keep her strong and able to do their work for them. "While he lived, the centre of the finance of the world may be said to have been his office in New Court" (B, Vol. X., p. 501). The British Government used the Rothschilds now as their unofficial envoys for confidential communications. Such is the power of Money that for twenty years Tsarist Russia, which the Jews always regarded as their worst enemy, employed Lionel Rothschild as its agent, although in 1861 Lionel refused to help to raise a loan for her. Lionel "actively co-operated with the Vienna Branch of his firm in directing the finances of the Austrian Empire" (B, Vol. X., p. 501). He was friend and counsellor of the Prince Consort.

The London house of Rothschild, under his management was particularly flourishing because it escaped the upheavals of the 1848 revolutions on the Continent.

Lionel Rothschild's principal tool was the perpetually hard-up Disraeli who, throughout his official career, worked unceasingly to obey his orders. Disraeli was an early crony of Lionel and an intimate friend of the Rothschild family and the Montefiores. On the marriage of Lionel's son, Leopold, Disraeli wrote to the latter (with Jewish delicacy) "I have always been of opinion that there cannot be too many Rothschilds" (L, p. 168). In 1845, Mrs. Disraeli desired to will all her property to Lionel Rothschild's daughter, Evelina. (M, p. 48).

In his novel *Coningsby*, Disraeli endeavoured to depict a world-powerful Jew whom he called Sidonia; this was a kind of composite portrait of Lionel Rothschild, Karl his uncle, and an imaginary individual whom one identifies without much difficulty with "Disraeli as Disraeli would like to have been." This "Sidonia" was a Sephardic Jew, heir to a loan-mongering world-wide business with family representatives in every capital, immensely rich, travelled, cultured to the last degree, and devoid of the ordinary humanities, esteeming intellect only, and managing the affairs of nations through his Money Power; and (which is the most revealing aspect of the author) "Sidonia" is firmly of opinion that Jews are a people superior to all others.

Disraeli was the principal agent through whom Lionel Rothschild, by granting financial and other favours to numerous traitors, at last and after many failures, secured "emancipation" for the Jews, with the right to sit in the House of Commons after taking a Jewish, not a Christian, oath. Lionel was first elected in 1847 as Member for the City of London, but as the House of Lords refused for years to pass Bills for Jewish Emancipation which had already got through the lower House, he was unable to take his seat. His constituency, however, returned him five times running. It was only in 1858 that he was enabled by law to take his oath in the Jewish form with his head covered. In 1850, he had actually the effrontery to try and bluff the House by substituting the words "So help me, God" for "on the true faith of a Christian," but was told to withdraw by the Speaker. The House of Commons has since been infested by the following members of the Rothschild family :—

Mayer Amschel, son of Nathan, for Hythe 1860-74.
Nathaniel, for Aylesbury, 1865-85.
Ferdinand, for Aylesbury, 1885-98.
Lionel Walter, for Aylesbury, 1899-1910.
Lionel Nathan, for Aylesbury, 1910-23.
James Edmond, for Isle of Ely, from 1929.

Lionel's brother Anthony Rothschild was the third professing Jew to be made a Baronet in 1846, and the first Rothschild to obtain a title in this country.

In his letters to his sister, Disraeli wrote how Lionel gave him advice and financial assistance; in questions affecting the emancipation of the Jews Lionel and Disraeli "were so much of the same opinion that the Conservative Minister almost always voted against his own party." (A, Vol. II., p. 445).

Disraeli and Lionel worked together against Russia. Disraeli was very friendly with Napoleon III., who mistrusted the Rothschild family. Over a trivial dispute in Palestine, Disraeli managed to persuade Napoleon to join with Britain in the Crimean War against Russia. Lionel Rothschild raised sixteen million pounds for the purpose of carrying out this war.

Doubtless, like other wars, it had been deliberately provoked, for the preceding year had seen an attempt upon Disraeli's part to form an alliance between Britain and France. (N, Chap. XIV.) Russia was always the Jews' most hated enemy, being the only country in Europe which steadfastly defended its interests against Jewish penetration by refusing to recognise Jews as Russians and compelling them to live and remain in particular localities known as the Pale of Settlement. It was always therefore the Jews' policy to impress upon Britain that Russia must never get an outlet into the Mediterranean and also that she was a constant danger to India. The probability is that if Russia had been able to take over Turkey, she would have gradually come under the influence of Western Civilisation by constant contact instead of following, as she eventually did, an Eastern Bolshevism. This contact the Jews have prevented. The Crimean War was a very definite step in the direction of isolating Russia from the rest of Europe.

Rothschild told Duke Ernst II. of Saxe-Coburg-Gotha that he would put any amount of money at his disposal for war with Russia. (O, Vol. II., page 143).

The Rothschilds underwrote great loans for France and Turkey, our allies. But they made huge profits in other ways out of this war. During the period following the fall of Sebastopol in September, 1855, and before the Armistice was arranged in February, 1856, rumours were set afloat that there would be no peace. This caused a panic on the Stock Exchange and a rush of sellers to "get out." The truth, i.e., that peace would follow, came from Sir G. H. Seymour, our Vienna diplomat, soon afterwards, and the funds rose five points in two days. "The Rothschilds and all the French, who were in the secret with Walewski, must have made untold sums." (K, 18th January, 1856). Walewski was the illegitimate son of Napoleon I.

No doubt it was the knowledge that through Disraeli he could exercise so much control over Napoleon III., that made Lionel display dismay (M, p. 144) over the surrender of the French Emperor to Prussia in 1870. Since the Crimean War and the American Civil War, the London Rothschilds were comparatively stagnant between 1865 and 1870 (L, p. 67), other firms getting a better "look-in."

In 1868, owing to the unsatisfactory results which often accompanied the lending of money abroad, a Council of Foreign Bondholders was formed with the object of influencing the Government to mould its policies so as to protect the creditors' interests. It was originally intended to make Lionel Rothschild the Chairman, but it happened that two of the foreign debtors who were behaving unsatisfactorily at the time were States for which the Rothschilds themselves had issued the loans (Z5, p. 316) ! So the appointment went elsewhere, although of course Rothschilds have always remained the most powerful influence behind the Council's actions.

One of the pet stories retailed by Jews to demonstrate how much England really owes to them is the one about the purchase of the Suez Canal shares. In 1875, the Khedive of Egypt, forced by financial stringency, was anxious to sell his interest in the Canal. Mr. F. Greenwood, Editor of the *Pall Mall Gazette*, received private advices that the shares might be acquired by England, and, patriotically refusing to make a journalistic " scoop " out of the information, hastened to Lord Derby with the news. Lord Derby consulted with the Jewish Prime Minister, Disraeli, and the latter bought the shares with money borrowed from his Rothschild masters. Parliament was not sitting at the time, and the amount loaned by the Rothschilds was four millions. It was, of course, a Jewish interest that Britain should get control over the Canal. The more power Britain exercised, the greater the strength of the Jews who really ruled her. Disraeli had written to Queen Victoria saying " We have scarcely time to breathe, we must carry the matter through ; " but he need never have gone to the Rothschilds at all. A letter in *The Times*, 20th March, 1930, tears the veil from the figure of the Jewish Patriot and discloses the unpleasant anatomy of this impossible conception. It was from Hon. G. M. Kinnaird, and said :—" When Disraeli announced to the House his purchase of the Suez Canal shares, my father, Hon. Arthur Kinnaird, M.P. for Perth, was seated next to the Governor of the Bank of England. On hearing Disraeli's statement that he had gone to the only people who could have advanced the money, the Governor of the Bank of England whispered to my father ' What a lie ! I could have given it to him in a minute.' " Thus, we know that the assistance of the Rothschilds was not needed. But we take it that the Jewish estimate that they made a clear £80,000 over the deal (L, p. 77), does not err in over-estimation of the profits. The Governor of the Bank at the time was H. H. Gibbs, later 1st Lord Aldenham.

Shortly afterwards, J. C. Biggar, M.P., asked in the House whether Nathaniel Rothschild, Lionel's son, at that time M.P. for Aylesbury, had not rendered himself liable to £500 fine for every time he had voted subsequent to the Suez Canal transaction, under the Act 22 George III., which prohibited M.P.'s from holding any office of profit under the Crown. To this, Nathaniel Rothschild answered with Jewish effrontery that the Act did not apply to him as he was not a *partner* in his father's firm ; this quibble was allowed to pass muster.

When Disraeli returned to England after signing the Treaty of Berlin which, among other things, arrested Russia's approach to the Mediterranean and put Jews on an equality with other people in the Balkan countries, one of the first to greet him on the decorated railway-platform was Sir Moses Montefiore, the old Jew jackal of the Rothschild connection.

During Lionel's lifetime it is estimated that he raised loans to the amount of sixteen hundred millions for the British Government.

He died in 1879, leaving three sons, Nathaniel, Alfred and Leopold, and two daughters who, according to the frequent custom of the family, married back into it. The sons were tutored by the Jew revolutionary Dr. M. M. Kalisch who had taken refuge in this country after participating in the 1848 convulsions on the Continent. This man also tutored the daughters of Lionel's brother, Sir Anthony Rothschild. (B, Vol. VII., p. 420).

           *   *   *   *   *   *

The three sons of course all inherited the title of Baron of Austria. But Nathaniel Rothschild was the first to become a Peer of England; this happened under Gladstone in 1885, the succession being as follows :—

     Nathaniel, 1st Baron, 1885.
     Lionel Walter, his son, 2nd Baron, 1915.
     Nathaniel Mayer Victor, the latter's nephew, 3rd Baron, 1937.

These will be the only members of the family that I shall refer to as Barons for the purpose of this book.

All Lionel's sons lived lives of great material magnificence, and their country seats were the meeting-places of the corrupt politicians and other schemers which democracy cast up to the surface. There was something to be got for nothing at the Rothschilds; or so it seemed at first; but it is plain that favours cannot be accepted frequently from the rich without return of any kind ! The reader will glean more about this in subsequent chapters dealing with the relations of the Rothschilds to certain important personages.

Nathaniel became the head of the firm in London, and maintained its intimacy with Disraeli; this, in spite of the fact that he represented himself to be a Gladstonian Liberal in Parliament, later becoming a Liberal Unionist. He took up a strong line against Russia, refusing to raise loans for her unless a promise was made that her protective ghetto laws should be abandoned. Nathaniel was the Rothschild who financed Rhodes in South Africa, a subject which is dealt with under the heading " Diamonds and Gold " (p. 61).

He also assisted the Vickers armament firm with new capital at the time of its extension. (Z 5, p. 334).

Nathaniel's brother, Alfred Rothschild, also bestowed favours on Disraeli, placing a suite of rooms at his disposal at Seamore Place, 1880 (L, p. 141). He became Austrian Consul-General in London and held this appointment at the outbreak of the Great War; and as, at that time (1914), the Secretary of the German Embassy in London was Albert Goldschmidt-Rothschild, grandson of William Rothschild of Frankfort, the family were in a good strategical political position.

From 1868 to 1889, Alfred was a Director of the Bank of England; he resigned because he had been discovered in a breach of faith, searching out and publishing the amount of profits made by a dealer who had sold him a French painting, these records being obtained from the Bank of England's books, the dealer being one of its depositors (L, p. 147).

From 1892 onwards, Alfred's house was the usual meeting-place of German Ambassadors seeking heart-to-heart talks with British politicians, and the *Jewish Chronicle* (14th Sept., 1934), wrote : " It was under his roof that Joseph Chamberlain met the German Ambassador to discuss matters of common interest. Subsequently, Sir Ernest Cassel on the one side, and Albert Ballin on the other, carried on the negotiations so far as to render possible the Haldane official visit to Berlin." Cassel and Ballin were of course both Jews, the former being the late King Edward VII.'s bosom friend, and the latter the Kaiser's adviser. The reader will find more about Haldane's intercourse with the Rothschilds on p. 50. He was Secretary for War at the time mentioned by the *Jewish Chronicle.* " At one period," says the Jew Roth, writing of Alfred Rothschild, " he used to go to 10, Downing Street every morning to see Asquith, another close friend, who set great store on his advice." (L, p. 159). Asquith was Prime Minister at Downing Street from 1908-15. In the war, Alfred paid daily visits also to Lord Kitchener at the War Office. (P, Vol. I., p. 134).

So well informed was Albert Rothschild, that when in the Russo-Japanese War the Japanese won their naval victory at Tsushima, Albert heard of it before the Japanese Embassy in London did. (*Daily Telegraph,* 31st May, 1934).

Alfred Rothschild never married, but he left the bulk of his immense fortune to Almina, Countess of Carnarvon, who is stated in *Burke's Peerage* to be the daughter of Mr. F. C. Wombwell. She is the mother of the present (6th) Earl of Carnarvon, and also of the wife of Sir B. C. Beauchamp, Bart., Lady Beauchamp's first names being Evelyn Leonora, the names of Alfred Rothschild's sisters.

Lionel Rothschild's third son, Leopold, interested himself in horse-racing and in Jewish communal affairs and his career calls for no special remark here.

In 1911, a hideous Ritual Murder was perpetrated by the Jews at Kiev, and the Rothschild legions were at once rushed up to the front to try and prevent punishment of the culprit. A " British Protest " was despatched to the Russian Government against " the revival " of the Ritual Murder charge; this was signed by the usual run of Arch-bishops and Bishops, together with Dukes and Earls including, of course, Lord Rosebery (who had married a Rothschild), and the inevitable Mr. A. J. Balfour; these people saw nothing improper in interfering with the course of justice before the accused Jew's trial was finished. But Baron Nathaniel Rothschild thought of a typical Jewish plan; he wrote to Cardinal Merry del Val, asking him to state authoritatively whether the Bull of Pope Innocent IV., dated 1247, was authentic, Lord Rothschild declaring that the Bull pronounced Jewish Ritual Murder to be " an unfounded and perfidious invention." When the Cardinal replied that the Bull was authentic, Rothschild tried to make out that Innocent IV. had denied the existence of such a thing as Jewish Ritual Murder. But, as shown in my book " *My Irrelevant Defence,* p. 44, the Bull does not contain any such statement as was imputed to it by Rothschild. Nevertheless, the Cardinal's reply has been exploited ever since by the Jews as confirming Rothschild's interpretation of the contents of the Bull, whereas all the Cardinal did was to acknowledge the authenticity of the Bull itself. Could anything be more typical of Jewish methods ?

With the object of looking after Jewish interests in the British

Empire, an "Anglo-Jewish Association" was formed in 1871, and Rothschilds, Sassoons, Montefiores and Goldsmids have always been the most prominent members. It works hand-in-glove with the Alliance Israelite Universelle (see p. 27) and has almost daily correspondence with the Central Committee of that organisation (B, Vol. I., p. 414).

The all-Jewish Masonic B'nai B'rith held the inaugural meeting of its first London Lodge at the house of Claude Montefiore, he being at that time (1909) President of the Anglo-Jewish Association. The first Council of the new B'nai B'rith Lodge had a Montefiore on its strength, and we may judge from this that B'nai B'rith will never deviate far from Rothschild policy in its secret interference with international politics.

The Presidency of the United Synagogue has been in Rothschild hands since Lionel Nathan Rothschild set the fashion, followed by Nathaniel, Leopold, Lionel Walter, and Lionel Nathan. During all this period, the Leader of the Jewish community in this country may be said to have been a Rothschild. The qualification for this leadership is obviously the ownership of great wealth. The Jews have now succeeded in mesmerising the Gentile community into accepting similar ideas concerning leadership.

Several incidents reveal the commanding position of the Rothschilds in the Great War 1914-18. In 1915, when Haig was made Commander-in-Chief "the first definite information that reached him with regard to his promotion, came, curiously enough, from his old friend Mr. Leopold de Rothschild, who was a regular correspondent. On Dec. 7th he wrote from London that 'all had been satisfactorily arranged'" (*Haig*, by Duff Cooper, 1935, p. 278). The mere Prime Minister, Asquith, informed Haig officially of his promotion in a letter marked "secret," dated the following day (8th Dec.) in which he ended thus :—" For the moment, all these changes ought to be kept private." This also is extracted from Duff Cooper's book.

Ever since this appointment, Haig acted with the Rothschild Sir Philip Sassoon as his private secretary.

Here we ask the reader to see p. 51 where the coming Dardanelles expedition was freely discussed among the Rothschilds long before it was actually attempted, and when the very idea was a secret of what Lord Bertie of Thame describes as "the inner circle." (P, Vol. I., p. 134).

Baron Nathaniel Rothschild died in 1915 ; his son, Baron Lionel Walter Rothschild resigned from his seat on the Tring Urban District Council because in 1916 it passed a resolution calling upon the Government to take immediate steps for the supervision of all aliens whether naturalised or not.

In 1919, a number of well-known Jews published an open letter in which they repudiated all sympathy with Bolshevism. The first signature to the letter was that of Baron Lionel Walter Rothschild. So far as he was concerned, there was no reason to disbelieve him. The Baku oil-wells of the Rothschilds were in grave jeopardy from Bolshevism and were ultimately confiscated by the Reds.

It is obvious, however, that the Rothschilds must have prayed for the success of the Jew Kerensky's Liberal Revolution, as they had always regarded the Tsars of Russia as their worst enemies. Actually, at the fall of the Tsar's Government, the London Rothschilds sent one million roubles to the Liberty Loan floated in St. Petersburg (L, p. 270) but they lost it all later when the Bolsheviks took over power.

The Rothschild attitude towards Bolshevism changes with the times; before Hitler took over the country, Czechoslovakia, which was under Rothschild control, was semi-sovietised and allied to Red Russia. So was France, under the Paris Rothschilds; she did all she could to bring about Bolshevism in Spain in opposition to General Franco. Now, in the Jewish War of revenge against the Nazis, we find the Rothschild agent, Sarraut, Minister of the Interior, taking measures to stamp out the Communist Party in France.

Gold from the Lena goldfields in Russia was sent frequently to the Rothschilds who refined it at the Royal Mint Refinery.

Lionel Nathan Rothschild, M.P. (Leopold's son) distinguished himself on 9th July, 1936, by attacking the position of the white man in Kenya. He moved a reduction of £100 on the Colonial Office vote to call attention to the Morris-Carter recommendations for ear-marking certain lands in that colony for European settlement. He waxed eloquent on the subject of the paramountcy of native interests over those of white men in our Colonies and Mandated Territories, apparently oblivious of the fact that in 1902 it had been seriously proposed to give large slices of the very best Kenya land for a Jewish National Home! No Jew was worrying about the paramountcy of native interests in Kenya then! The amusing story how the Jews were prevailed upon ultimately to give up the idea of Kenya as a National Home is told in *The Fascist*, August, 1935.

According to the *Daily Express* of 28th April, 1937, the present (3rd) Baron Victor Rothschild was asked by W. Hickey where he would live when the lease of the Rothschild Piccadilly home fell in? The answer was "Nowhere probably; I just don't know. *Not till after the war anyway.*" Thus it seems that the Rothschilds had made up their minds that there should be a war. And there was. Pure coincidence, of course. But it was quite far-seeing: two-and-a-half years! Remarkable.

Among the stockbroking firms which work for the Rothschilds is Vickers da Costa, a partner in which is Mr. Winston Churchill's brother, Mr. J. S. S. Churchill. Another of these firms is Cazenove Akroyd & Greenwood, and it is stated in *Men of the Reign*, 1885, p. 171-2, that Philip Cazenove (1799-1880) became prosperous in the Stock Exchange because of the "powerful interest of the founder of the house of Rothschild," by whom Nathan was obviously meant. Cazenove became a munificent supporter of Church charities! We may take it that Cazenove spells Rothschild, and it is well known that the name Churchill stands for "the Jews," from Solomon Medina in the early 18th century who paid £6,000 a year for the information the Duke of Marlborough (a Churchill) exchanged for that sum in the wars on the continent, to Barney Baruch on whose doorstep Winston broke his leg on his last visit to the U.S.A. Winston Churchill is thus not altogether an inappropriate First Sea Lord in a war against the Jews' chief enemy Herr Adolf Hitler.

Until 1938, the Rothschilds had a large interest in the multiple shops of Woolworth's Chain Stores, amounting to two-and-a-quarter million ordinary and 4,800,000 preference shares. The ordinary shares were sold in 1938 through the Jew firm Philip Hill & Partners.

In late years, an absurd film has been boosted in Europe and America called "The House of Rothschild," in which Nathan Rothschild is depicted as the chief of Britain's patriots, whilst the Duke of Wellington appears as a sort of clown. The absurdity of the immigrant Jew, Nathan Rothschild, uncultured, never able even to speak decent English, and obviously incapable of thinking like an Englishman, being a *Patriot* is clear to anyone uncontaminated by such ridiculous propaganda. The first night performance of this shameless travesty of history was arranged by Mr. Anthony Rothschild and his wife (who is very active in pushing forward Jewish propaganda films), the Jewesses the Marchioness of Reading and Mrs. Israel Moses Sieff. It was acknowledged in the press to be pure Jewish propaganda for the Gentile.

Before leaving the English scene, the development of the Alliance Assurance Co. which we have seen was started by Nathan Rothschild, calls for a few sentences. Lloyds and the Alliance are now united. Lord Wardington, Chairman of Lloyds is a Director of the Alliance. Sir Austin Harris, Deputy-chairman of Lloyds, and a Director of the Commercial Union Assurance Co. has a son married to the grand-daughter of Nathaniel Rothschild. Nathaniel and Lionel Walter Rothschild were both Chairmen of the Alliance in succession. The Alliance Assurance Co. has the controlling interest of the Rio Tinto Company which manages the Rothschild copper mines in Spain (see p. 58), the Chairman of which is Sir Auckland Geddes. No wonder the Geddes family gets on ! The other Directors of the Alliance Assurance Co. include representatives of the Bank of England, of Baring Bros., and the Oil Jew, Lord Bearsted of the Shell Co. and of M. Samuel & Co.

When Nathaniel Rothschild was one day looking through new risks undertaken by the Company, he found (L, p. 249) that his son, Lionel Walter, had actually insured his father's life for £200,000, partly in the Company. This was too much for Nathaniel, who discouraged his son's participation in Rothschild business thereafter. But the Jew C. Roth evidently thought it was a very smart bit of work, or he would surely not have recorded it in his book.

Four per cent. Industrial Dwellings is a Company formed by Nathaniel Rothschild in 1885, and has an all-Jewish Directorate to-day.

CHAPTER III.

WE must go back 130 years to find out how the Rothschilds became the Government of France, because it was in 1811 that Amschel Rothschild (the first) sent his son James to help in carrying out some particularly dirty work in Paris, necessitating the co-operation of his other son, Nathan in England.

James Rothschild was not commissioned to start a Branch of the Rothschild house at once; he was sent secretly from Frankfort to Paris to collect coin to aid the Duke of Wellington in his expected advance from Spain through southern France (B, Vol. X., p. 494), a proceeding which of course was an example of the utmost duplicity and treachery to the nation which he afterwards came to control. He received bullion sent from England by his brother Nathan, importing it at Dunkirk, passing it through to Paris and exchanging it there for paper of Paris Banks which was then sent on to Wellington in Spain to cash with Spanish and other banks as requisite. James also smuggled French bullion to Holland, whence it was shipped to Wellington's headquarters.

The reader will be surprised, perhaps, that such work was possible under the eyes and nose of Napoleon. Actually, Napoleon's Marshal Davoust, Military Governor of Hamburg, acting on the advice of his police, warned him against the activities of the Rothschild family, whilst the Paris Prefect of Police advised the arrest of James Rothschild himself. (A, Vol. I., p. 137-9). The Police Commissioner at Mainz reported also the intimate relations of Amschel Rothschild with Dalberg, Napoleon's representative at Frankfort, already described (see p. 10).

How was it then that James Rothschild was not arrested and executed as a spy by Napoleon? It is all very simple and Rothschildian. The fact is that the French Finance Minister, Count von Mollien, found that James Rothschild's advice and early reports of events, to say nothing of the frequency with which von Mollien found it convenient to get Rothschild to execute commissions for him, made James's arrest inadvisable! (A, Vol. I., p. 139). In other words, James was "following in father's footsteps" by sweetening the officials of Napoleon; he could defy arrest.

At last, in 1817, the Paris Rothschild offices were opened.

In 1822, James was made Austrian Consul-General in Paris. This of course was done through the influence of his brother Solomon over Metternich in Vienna (see Chapter IV.) He became an Austrian Baron together with his brothers. James flourished under the Bourbon rule, assisting the French kingdom with loans and financial advice.

But he kept open a line of retreat. When the dynastic Bourbons were expelled by the Revolution of 1830, Rothschild was only a temporary loser, because he had long ago wormed himself by monetary assistance into the favour of Louis Philippe, Duke of Orleans, who then came to the throne. By 1832, therefore, James had weathered the crisis, and was again in full favour of a French King. Louis Philippe made James his adviser, although Thiers, his Minister, did not like it ; but Thiers himself owed money to Rothschild so his opposition was feeble ! When Thiers wished to help Mehmet Ali in Egypt, and Rothschild advised the opposite course, it was Thiers who had to resign ! This was in 1840, and very recently Moses Montefiore had been to visit Mehmet Ali and the Sultan of Turkey with huge bribes which effected the release (without re-trial) of a number of Jews condemned for a frightful ritual murder of a French priest at Damascus, and obtained favours for Jews under Turkish rule.

James Rothschild was now the great power in Paris. Metternich wrote in 1845 (A, Vol. II., p. 245) " By reason of natural (sic !) causes which I cannot regard as good or as moral, the House of Rothschild is a much more important influence in French affairs than the Foreign Office of any country, except perhaps England. The great motive force is their money. People who hope for philanthrophy, and who have to suppress all criticism under the weight of gold, need a great deal of it. The fact of corruption—that practical element, in the fullest sense of the word—in the modern representative system, is recognised quite openly." The German Minister in Paris, Von Arnim, whom Disraeli stated to be a Jew (Coningsby, Book IV., Chapter XV.), suggested that few Governments were in a position to say that they did not bear the golden chains of the House of Rothschild (A, Vol. II., p. 246, quoting from Gesichte Frankreichs, Hillebrand II., 646). Think, reader, what that meant.

The poet Heine, who was financed by James Rothschild and took hospitality freely from him, said that James " was the first to perceive the worth of Cremieux, who became his advocate " (Lutelia, Part I., Karpeles edition, VI., 385). It was, in fact, James Rothschild who first brought Cremieux into prominence, and therefore it is necessary to explain who Cremieux was, so that we may understand the motives of his patron. Isaac Adolphe Cremieux was a Jew ; he was not only a Grand Orient Freemason, but "rose " to become a member of the Supreme Council of a super-Masonry of 90 degrees, called the Rite of Mizraim, becoming Grand Master in 1869. It was Cremieux who formed the Alliance Israelite Universelle, one of the most powerful organisations in the world for the extension of Jewish power over Gentile nations ; this body was represented officially at the Berlin Congress (1878) and succeeded in getting the Powers to force upon Rumania, Servia and Bulgaria the emancipation of the Jews in those countries, although Rumania slithered out of the obligation. The Alliance Israelite Universelle has frequently interfered with justice on behalf of Jewish criminals guilty of Ritual Murder, and it was Cremieux who accompanied Moses Montefiore in 1840 to bribe the Khedive and the Sultan as described already.

Cremieux had an adopted son, a Jew called Gambetta (identified as a Jew by Archduke Albert of Austria, a prominent Jesuit who knew all the leading figures in active politics ; this was in a letter dated 5th Jan., 1883, quoted by Crown Prince Rudolph in a letter dated 13th of the same month to the political Jew journalist Morris Szeps, see My Life and History, by Bertha Szeps, 1938, p. 52). He did all he could to push forward this Jew, Gambetta. It is necessary for the reader to note, then, that Cremieux was James Rothschild's man, and that Gambetta was Cremieux's man, for we shall meet them again very soon.

Returning to James, concessions obtained from King Louis Philippe had made him the Railway "King" of France, and he had a number of Jewish bankers acting as his jackals, particularly Emil Pereire. It is to be remarked, however, that the whole of these railway enterprises in France were due to English initiative and energy (R, Vol. X., p. 786).

Then came the Revolution of 1847-8 which was copied all over the Continent with more or less success. James Rothschild's tout, Cremieux, had taken a leading part in bringing it about, and it was most definitely a Masonic revolution. Louis Philippe fled the country. James himself was at Cremieux's back, expecting to be able to control the revolutionaries through him at least as well as he had controlled Louis Philippe. But they had not reckoned with the strength of the mob, which, having genuine grievances enough against the old regime, refused to accept the provisional Government which the Freemasons had formed and in which Cremieux himself was Minister for Justice. The Minister of Finance in this provisional government was a friend of Rothschild's, a Jew called Goudcheaux who was there to protect Rothschild interests during the change over. The mob, however, formed its own republican government in opposition to the Rothschild combine, and the latter had to consent to a sort of amalgamation with these hostile elements. Goudcheaux had to resign, and James was left in a very awkward position; the mob-revolutionaries knew that he had been the intimate adviser of Louis Philippe and that he was always ready to back both sides of any cause; he was made to pay heavily for his personal safety and his villa at Suresnes was pillaged. The new Finance Minister, Ledru-Rollin, extorted money from James with threats of vengeance if he did not pay up (A, Vol. II., p. 263). It was a thin time for the Paris Rothschild.

Even when Louis Napoleon, recommended by Cremieux himself as a candidate, became President, James Rothschild had to take a back seat, because, once in the saddle, Louis Napoleon, knowing how easily a Rothschild changed his coat, made it clear to the horror of Rothschild and Cremieux that he was going to rely upon other Jew bankers, Fould and Oppenheim, and not upon the Rothschilds. Even the Jew Pereire found that it would pay him to side against Rothschild and with Louis Napoleon.

Cremieux, finding that the Rothschilds were turned down by Louis Napoleon, turned against him, and when thrown out of office by Louis Napoleon's assumption of the title of Emperor Napoleon III., he became his mortal enemy and worked up his Masons to overthrow him.

They had to make the best of a bad job. Cremieux pushed forward his adopted Jew son, Gambetta, who became the chief of the Left Wing against Napoleon III. What sort of a man was this? Let us see what the Archduke Albert, in his letter already cited (see p. 27) has to say about this Rothschild-Cremieux product:—" He gambled and stole wherever he could." Napoleon III. lasted much longer than the Rothschilds hoped, in spite of Gambetta, and they were only able to use him through Disraeli, who was friendly with him ; the Rothschilds had generally to be content with playing second fiddle to him. Undoubtedly, through Disraeli, they pushed him into alliance with Britain for the Crimean War.

James Rothschild died in 1868, and the Paris office was taken over by his son, Alphonse. He had three other sons, Solomon, Gustav and Edmond, and all held the Austrian title of Baron. Together they inherited an estate estimated at 2,000 million francs.

The Franco-Prussian War finished Napoleon III., and when he abdicated it was the Rothschild-Cremieux agent Gambetta who became Minister of the Interior to the Republic, and, by virtue of Rothschild money, its dictator. It was Gambetta who conducted the negotiations on behalf of defeated France with Bismarck, who, in turn was advised by another Jew, a former revolutionary of 1848, Ludwig Bamberger, a friend of Cremieux, who had for four years been manager of the Paris Branch of the Jew Bank of Bischoffsheim & Goldschmidt; whilst Alphonse " became head of the syndicate of French bankers which guaranteed the payment of the indemnity of five milliard francs by France to Germany." (B, Vol. X., p. 498). Everything was in the Rothschild grip again, so they were unshaken by the Franco-Prussian War. They financed the Commune of 1871, and the residence of Alphonse was, most significantly, untouched by communist mobs, (A, Vol. II., p. 425) although it was in a particularly exposed position where the Rue de Rivoli joins the Place de la Concorde in which fighting was intense. We have already seen how, leading up to the Franco-Prussian War, Alphonse Rothschild in Paris and Bleichroder (Bismarck's Jew) in Berlin were acting as intelligence officers (see p. 12), doubtless shaping their information to bring about the downfall of Napoleon III.

Their tool, Gambetta (quoting again the Archduke Albert) owed his power as virtual dictator to " his high position as a Freemason, to his Jewish origin, and to his will-power, all of which secured him the allegiance of all Freemasons, all Jews, and all those who do not know how to help themselves." The Press, practically all Jewish, supported him. France became again a paradise for the Rothschilds.

Alphonse Rothschild interested himself particularly in electrical development and petrol, with as much monopoly power in those spheres as could be achieved.

The politician Leon Say (1826-96) was a good example of a Rothschild-controlled politician. His first step in life was given him by Alphonse Rothschild who made him administrator of the Northern Railway. (Z5, p. 165). Subsequently, he was Finance Minister from 1872 to 1880 and again in 1882, " the autocratic ruler of the French finances " (R, Vol. XXIV., p. 275). No doubt there were scores of similar cases.

With the aid of the wife of the Russian Finance Minister, a Jewess, Alphonse arranged a loan for the hated Tsar, taking the standpoint that thereby the Tsar would be more likely to be sweetened towards the Jews and the repeal of the ghetto laws in Russia than by withholding and refusing the loan, that being the policy of the Rothschild in London. (A, Vol. II., p. 443).

During the Great War 1914-18, the Rothschilds of Paris made enormous profits from their control of nickel, copper and lead mines, the shady transactions being described under these heads (see p.p. 57-58). It is interesting to know that Mme. Henri de Rothschild lent the ground-floor of her house for the Inter-Allied Officers' Club.

In Paris, a Central Consistory of the Alliance Israelite Universelle is a permanent feature, a sort of Sanhedrin or Parliament of World Jewry. As might be expected, the Rothschilds dominate it; in 1920 three Baron Rothschilds were on its strength, namely Edmond, Robert and Edouard, the last named being the President. It is to be noted that on attaining the 18th Degree, a Grand Orient Mason automatically becomes if not a member at least a supporter of the Alliance Israelite Universelle. (F, Vol. II., p. 487).

When Trotsky escaped to the United States in 1934 it was through a western port, disguised as an employee of a Paris Rothschild bank (Q, p. 58).

This followed two secret meetings in France, one in 1933 between Litvinoff, Trotsky, Baron Rothschild and R. Moley, once a lecturer at the Rand School for Social Science, New York; the other in May, 1934, between Litvinoff, Barney Baruch, Trotsky and Baron Maurice de Rothschild. (Q, p. 112), All are Jews except Moley.

It is part of the Jewish scheme to control all political movements, if they can, not excluding Fascism. Fascists should be careful to make sure that their leaders are clear of all Jewish and Masonic influence. Never mind what they say. Find out what they are. In 1935, Col. de la Rocque started a " patriotic " ' movement in France called the Croix de Feu and it had endless funds which secured it a large following ; its first charitable function was held in the grounds of a Rothschild mansion ! Jews were taken in as members of this precious organisation, and it published its policy in a book *The Fiery Cross* in which it poured odium and ridicule upon the German Nazis and described Bolshevism without any mention that both its origin and establishment are Jewish. This " Fascist " movement had a Jew Carvalho as Secretary and a Jew Wormser as Financial Adviser.

Alphonse Rothschild died in 1905, and his son, Edouard, took over the Paris business house.

The real Government of France is not a democracy; " R.F." does not really mean Republique Francaise, but Rothschild Freres. Financial pressure can always be exercised by the Rothschilds upon any Government of France, whatever its political complexion. This is done through the Banque de France of which a Rothschild is always the principal Regent, working hand-in-glove with the armament men, Wendel and the Marquis de Vogue who both represent the Schneider-Creusot arms firm.

It is of great interest to note that on 5th Oct., 1935, when Italy was attacking Abyssinia, both the *Daily Telegraph* and the *Financial Times* reported that a loan, one-third from the Rothschilds, of eight million pounds had been granted to the Credit Italiano Bank ; this was denied two weeks later ! But on 21st Oct., the *Internationale Presse Agentur* stated that the French House of Rothschild had given Italy a credit of 750 million francs. No wonder Britain could not get France to apply

" sanctions " against Italy under the Covenant of the League of Nations ! Baron Franchetti, the chief " Italian " expert on Abyssinia, who was killed in an aeroplane accident on his way there, was the grandson of Wilhelm Rothschild !

It is also worthy of report that Baron Maurice Rothschild was at Geneva during the League of Nations sanctions conference, and the *Daily Express*, 14th October, published a photograph of him chatting with the President of the Committee after the final meeting of the conference.

Henri Rothschild, a grandson of the Nathaniel who was the son of Nathan, lives in Paris and is a playwright, his pen-name being Andre Pascal.

CHAPTER IV.

THE VIENNA HOUSE.

IN Austria, Count Metternich, the most prominent figure in European politics of the time, with the exception of Napoleon, and through whose instrumentality the latter had been offered the hand of Marie Louise of Austria, became Foreign Minister in 1809. His reputation has been handed down to us through Judaised history books as that of a " reactionary," whereas we may now, in 1939, knowing where democracy has led us, realise that Metternich had a very far-seeing intelligence and recognised how the plausible democratic theories which sprang everywhere into life during his long period of activity must inevitably bring down civilisation itself. So he was ever an enthusiastic opponent of the secret Masonic societies which he knew were behind all the revolutionary tendencies of his day. He believed in the rule of an aristocracy, but was so confident in that belief that he seemed to imagine that such things as domestic morals were only for the crowd and not for him. Nevertheless, he was an upright man according to his lights, and never took bribes from Rothschilds or anyone else. He had, however, a singular capacity in trusting the wrong men; he made Frederick von Gentz his secretary and adviser, and, as we have seen (see p. 13) this Jew was one of the Illuminati, and had no moral sense at all, but was an intellectual voluptuary who would and did take bribes from anyone to finance his expensive orgies. It is curious how the fact that von Gentz was a Jew has been overlooked by so many writers who otherwise recognised his subversive influence over Austrian affairs. Disraeli acknowledged him as a " child of Israel " (S, Chapter XXIV.) whilst the Jew Grunwald reveals the fact that his first name was really not Frederick but Muasso (T, p. 194).

" It was to von Gentz that the Rothschilds largely owed their position with Metternich " says Corti (A, Vol. II., p. 69). This introduction dated from 1813, the year in which Metternich abandoned Napoleon and threw his weight into the coalition of powers against him. After the Battle of Waterloo, the Frankfort House of Rothschild began to do large-scale business with the Austrian Goverment, and (his father being dead some years) Solomon Rothschild was sent to establish permanently a branch of the Rothschild business in Vienna. This was in 1816. It was obvious that the Grand Orient Mason, Solomon Rothschild, would find much in common with the Illuminatus von Gentz. Solomon was already immensely experienced in the crooked ways of finance and had travelled widely in Europe for the Frankfort house. Gentz's ways of life were expensive and he always needed money; he never hid the fact that he took bribes where he could get them. He used to exchange political information to the Rothschilds, which would allow them to rig markets to their profit, in return for "loans" of the kind that never require to be repaid. (A, Vol. II., p. 69).

No doubt it was due to the influence of von Gentz that Metternich's librarian was also a Jew, named Schiel. It was a tragedy and almost inexplicable, that Metternich, surrounded with Jews as he became, what with his Jewish secretary, his Jewish librarian, and his Jewish financier, never became Jew-wise. I ask, in all seriousness, whether, in view of the antecedents of von Gentz and of Solomon Rothschild in Illuminism and Masonry respectively, mesmerism could have been employed against Metternich? Although Metternich accepted personal loans from Rothschild, these were repaid with fair interest, and no one charges Metternich with corruption by money.

One of the first loans arranged for the Austrian Government by the Rothschilds was a "lottery loan" which was remarkable from the facts (1) that the subscribers to it were not informed that another loan would soon follow and (2) that the terms were exceedingly onerous for Austria. A Police Report dated 1st May, 1820, in the Vienna Police Archives says of it:—"The whole transaction is felt to be a shameful Jewish ramp which has been arranged between the Rothschilds and the Crown Agent Joel." (A, Vol. I., p. 246). This Joel is later referred to (A, Vol. I., p. 246) as "Joel or Joelson."

Here I insert a curious statement taken from *Tour to Constantinople* by the Marquess of Londonderry, published 1842, Vol. I., p. 59, which, speaking of Prince Metternich, says "After the death of the first princess, in 1819 or 1820, I believe, the Prince married a very beautiful girl, the daughter of 'Mr. Joelson.' " I cannot explain this mystery, as the second wife of Metternich is elsewhere recognised as Baroness von Leykam, Countess of Beylstein.

Solomon thrived so well in Vienna that very soon, where money was concerned, Austria under Metternich was in Rothschild hands. In 1821, Solomon's brother was sent to open a branch of the house at Naples which was in Austrian occupation, and Metternich, who became Chancellor, made Solomon's other brother James in Paris his Austrian Consul-General! Then, next year he had all five of old Amschel Rothschild's sons made Barons of Austria! Metternich was acting like Solomon's clerk, and he a convinced and uncompromising aristocrat!

This was the period of Power with the Rothschilds. Between 1817 and 1848 it is estimated that the loans issued by the Rothschild family amounted to 131 million pounds. (B, Vol. X., p. 495). The musty details of these loans will not interest my Aryan readers and I do not cater for others. In 1839, Solomon had secured a mortgage on all the Austrian Lloyd Co.'s ships in return for a loan.

"In the early stages of its existence, the Austrian house of Rothschild had a large money-lending business with the mediated and impoverished nobility of the Austrian Empire. Loans to the amount of 24,521,000 guilden being on record." (B, Vol. X, p. 495). So Solomon Rothschild was never in need of Gentile traitors to do his work. By 1840, Solomon's wealth and its ostentatious display dazzled Vienna society and he was not only sought after for his money but even socially as well.

Metternich appointed the Rothschilds over the head of his own Paris Ambassador as the principal channel of communication between himself and the French Cabinet. When the question arose of appointing Lionel Rothschild Austrian Consul-General in London, Metternich supported this course because, he said, otherwise the Rothschild family might become hostile to Austria! (A, Vol. II., p. 170). Thus, the chief upholder of the aristocratic principle and the virtual head of one of the most powerful States in Europe had become the frightened servant of the Rothschilds who could blackmail him into bestowing on a member of the family a vital diplomatic appointment.

Needless to say, the Rothschilds extorted from Metternich many privileges for the Jews in Austria and wherever Austria had influence. It was Metternich who, in 1833, prevented the Papal States from re-establishing the ghetto for Jews; and in 1844, Solomon Rothschild secured for the Jews the right of holding landed estate in Austria.

Considering that Metternich wished to interfere by force against Louis Philippe in France, who, as supplanter of the rightful line of Bourbon, represented to him the revolutionary spirit in Europe, and considering that Louis Philippe's regime was still supported by the flourishing Rothschilds, it must be surely plain to all that it was the Rothschilds who ruled the destinies of Europe and dedicated it to democratic degeneration. Metternich did not foresee that Louis Philippe's rule would itself come to an end by revolution.

"Following the policy of the House of Rothschild in other countries, where it obtained privileges for the Jews in return for loans—in Rome, the abolition of the ghetto, and in England, Jewish emancipation—Solomon obtained from Metternich concessions to the Jews in legislation. It was he who influenced the Chancellor to take a favourable stand in the Damascus blood-accusation case of 1840." So says the Jew Grunwald (T, p. 228-9). This Ritual Murder is described in my book *My Irrelevant Defence*, p. 24. The result of Solomon's efforts was an unsuccessful attempt of the Austrian Consul at Damascus to bribe the French Consul to withdraw the charge of ritual murder against the Jews.

As the Rothschilds had such complete control over Austria, they were not unduly incommoded by the death of their tool, the corrupt secretary of Metternich, the Jew von Gentz.

The spread of the 1848 revolutionary spirit to Austria caused Metternich to fly for his safety; Solomon Rothschild's house in Vienna was looted, and he also fled the country, never to return, for he died in 1855. Not until reaction had set in, did Metternich dare to return, and then Solomon's son, Anselm Rothschild, who was then Austrian Consul-General at Frankfort, re-established the Rothschild business, to be followed at his death in 1874 by his son, Albert Solomon Rothschild. This Rothschild was the first in Austria to be granted the privilege of attending Courts. Albert followed the policy of interference with European politics which Solomon had established as a Rothschild practice, for we find Professor Goldwin Smith (Professor of Modern History at Oxford, and later of English History at Cornell University) writing on the alarms of the Russo-Turkish War of 1877 : " We were on the brink of a war with Russia which would have involved the whole of the Empire. . . . . The Jewish interest throughout Europe, with the Jewish press of Vienna as its chief organ, was doing its utmost to push us in " (*Nineteeth Century* Magazine, Oct., 1881, p. 494-5).

The Jewish press of Vienna carried out the orders of the Rothschilds.

Albert Rothschild was the largest stockholder in the Northern Railway, a concern which Solomon had the concession to develop by means of a public company in 1836. Later, it was nationalised. He held a similar position in the Southern Railway which the Rothschilds bought from the State on favourable terms.

By 1899, Albert possessed "alone about a quarter of the land in Bohemia (seven times as much as the Imperial Family) without counting that he possesses equally in other provinces, in Lower Austria, Moravia, Silesia and in Hungary " (*L'Autriche Juive*, by F. Trocase, 1899, published by A. Pierret, Paris).

The Vienna House now found most of its time taken up rather with the administration of its wealth than in the department of banking ; Albert became Chief Shareholder in the Credit Anstalt and when he died, 1911, he left 50 million pounds. His sons, Louis and Eugene emerge into our contemporary history. It was during Albert's administration that he did not shrink from using his financial power, at a time when debt-conversion was a serious matter to Hungary, to demand peremptorily that the Hungarian Government should not only withdraw the charges of murder against a Jew (the well-known Ritual Murder case of Tisza Eszlar) but that two Public Prosecutors who had been bribed to discredit the Judge at the trial should be decorated ! This was done via his Budapest representative Goldschmidt (U, p. 30).

Until closed down by Hitler, the Vienna Rothschild House never hesitated to influence affairs in other countries ; when Kamal Ataturk, the Turkish dictator, was about to execute for treason the ex-Finance Minister, a crypto-Jew called Djavid Bey, " a number of great financial concerns, including the banking houses of the Rothschilds in Vienna and London, had tried to persuade the English and French Governments and the leading newspapers in both countries to use all their influence to make a personal appeal for Djavid," (V, p, 276). Observe the words " persuade " and " personal," and guess what form the persuasion took in the case of both Newspapers and Governments ! The persuasion was such that the French Government sent the Grand Orient Freemason Sarraut to Angora to do the "personal " pleading with

34

Kamal. This Sarraut is Minister for the Interior in the French War Cabinet of 1940!

The chief coal mines and iron-works at Witkowitz, in Moravia were owned by the Austrian Rothschilds in partnership with the Jew von Gutmann, and by 1939 the value of the assets of the Company they formed was estimated at anything between ten and forty million pounds.

"Czechoslovakia" is only another way of spelling Rothschild.

It is important, therefore, to note the close collaboration between that country and the Soviets, because this could not have developed without the sanction of the Rothschilds. One should get into the habit of associating the names of Masaryk and Benes rather with the Rothschilds than with "Czechoslovakia" if one is to see clearly through the fog of international politics.

It is estimated that by 1933, Barons Louis and Eugene Rothschild between them owned more than half the financial and industrial property in Austria. All their estates were confiscated by the Germans in 1938.

The Bohmische Escompte Bank in Prague was a Rothschild bank, the largest in the country.

The Credit Anstalt was formed by Anselm Rothschild after Solomon's death; its original object was to keep the non-Rothschild Credit Mobilier out of Vienna. Anselm roped the Princes Furstenberg, Schwartzenberg and Auersberg, and Count Chotek into the racket.

Owing to the impossible state of affairs in Austria due to her dismemberment after the Great War, various Banks began to crash, and by the end of 1930, the Credit Anstalt itself was in difficulty, its losses amounting to its entire share capital and reserves. The Austrian National Bank and the Rothschilds stepped in to try and save it by a huge loan, but were too late, and the flight of financial capital from Austria became a rout. Then *you*, gentle reader, were shoved into the firing line, for the Bank of England advanced £4,400,000 to the Austrian Banks, and this amount was subsequently repaid to the Bank of England, not by Austria, but . . . . by the Treasury, which means YOU, the British tax-payer! (Do you *still* believe that democracy means self-government, or is it Government by Rothschild Jews?) President Hoover of the U.S.A. then proposed a moratorium of one year on international debts and that cost us, according to the Chancellor of the Exchequer Philip Snowden, not less than £11,000,000! Then the panic reached Germany (pre-Nazi) and her international creditors rushed to her assistance with loans and more loans; but the German Banks smashed up in spite of it.

As a further result of this continental panic, the people who held over £400,000,000 foreign short-term funds on loan in Britain began to call for their money, and that began the drain upon the Bank of England that bled her of gold, and caused intense depression in business with accompanying increased unemployment, which the Government tried to counter by quack remedies; the Banque of France came to the rescue for a time, but the Bank of England ultimately had to surrender by accepting foreign loans; first of £45,000,000, then of £80,000,000!

During all this time, Sir Otto Niemeyer and Louis Rothschild were co-Directors of the Credit Anstalt, and the former was a Director of the Bank of England.

Thus, just as the world is now (1940) at war against Germany with the single object of saving the Jews (for no other object is demonstrable for Britain and Germany to be at war) so, to save Rothschild credit in Austria, the whole world has had to increase its indebtedness to the usurers and to suffer from the resulting money-shortage by semi-paralysis of business !

" England saves Austria ; " " France saves England ; " these were the catch-cries of the day. All that really happened was that the British tax-payer saved the Austrian Rothschilds, and then the Paris Rothschilds saved the Bank of England from bankruptcy, leaving the British tax-payer still paying, and that under a reduced standard of living !

And that is a good note on which to end this Chapter on the Rothschilds who did business in Austria, for you see, my reader, that their work has affected *your* standard of living in Great Britain, and that you are now at war with Hitler, the very man who brought the alien power of the Vienna Rothschilds to an end ! Can you now guess why you are at war ?

CHAPTER V.

THE NAPLES HOUSE.

THE Rothschilds obtained their first footing in Naples when Metternich of Austria sent troops to occupy the town in 1821, to support its King against revolutionary upheaval caused by the Carbonari, a masonic secret society. Metternich persuaded the Rothschilds to raise a loan to pay for the costs of the invasion and upkeep of the Austrian troops, and this was actually arranged to be done as a loan to Naples, not to Austria ! For this purpose, Karl Rothschild, Solomon's brother and old Amschel's son, who had already done considerable service in the Frankfort House, was sent in that year to Naples.

Naturally in the double role of a member of the Rothschild family and a servant of Metternich, he soon became very powerful, and " contrived to make himself indispensible to the Neapolitan Court in financial matters " (A, Vol. I., p. 297). This was all the easier as the costs of the occupation of the Kingdom by Austrian troops ruined the State and made it more subject to the favours of the Rothschilds in the matter of loans.

The Papal States were among those to appeal to the Jew for loans, who, in 1831, lent them sixteen million francs, whilst his patron Metternich tried to get the ghetto gates in Rome abolished ; but the Pope re-erected them. This was followed in 1845 by a smaller loan, but it is to be noted to their credit that neither of the two Popes, Gregory XVI. or Pius IX., who were reigning at these periods, were Jew-friendly on that account. It was Gregory who decorated the anti-Jewish Gougenot des Mousseaux as a reward for writing his work exposing the nature of the Jew and which exposes the practice of Ritual Murder by them ; and it was Pius who refused audience to the Jew Montefiore on his journey back from bribing the Khedive and the Sultan over the Jewish Ritual Murders of Damascus and of Rhodes in 1840. (U, p. 23 seq.). Nevertheless, Karl Rothschild obtained the Papal order of St. George (!) with the privilege of kissing the Pope's hand instead of his toe ! (A, Vol. II., p. 51). Faugh !

When Pius IX. had sought safety from the revolutionaries of 1848, he needed Rothschild loans to enable him to regain his temporal power : they did not grant him the loan until he promised to pull down the ghetto walls in Rome and establish freedom of movement and abolition of special taxes for Jews ; this he refused to do until 1850, when the loan of thirty-three million francs was granted to him, on that condition. Payments of interest soon got into arrears (*Daily Telegraph*, 2nd Nov., 1935), which may be the reason that long after the Rothschild House in Naples had been closed down, the Rothschilds remained guardians of the Papal Treasure !

When Louis Napoleon came to be Emperor of France in 1852, both he and Cavour in Sardinia were strenuously endeavouring to free their respective countries from Rothschild influence, although they still resorted to Jews ; Louis Napoleon started the Credit Mobilier in 1852, whilst Cavour, whose secretary was the Jew Artom, employed the Jewish Bank of Hambro.

Karl's influence was therefore prevented from spreading too widely, and when Garibaldi conquered Naples and united Italy under Victor Emanuel, the former King of Sardinia, the Naples House of Rothschild was closed down (1861), and Karl retired to Paris where he remained in close familiarity with the Bourbon Royal Family of Naples who had gone there to live after their dethronement.

In Paris, the ex-King and Queen of Naples were on intimate social terms with Alphonse Rothschild (*My Past*, by Countess Larisch, Chapter VIII.).

Rothschilds have married into several Italian families of Jews ; thus, Anselm Rothschild's daughter married Baron Raymondo Franchetti in 1858, with descendants ; Gustav Rothschild's daughter married Baron Emanuel Leonino in 1896, and in the same year the daughter of Jas. Edward Rothschild married Baron David Leonino.

CHAPTER VI.

THE AMERICAN HOUSE.

ROTHSCHILD influence in the United States of America is of very long standing, but there is no reason to believe the story that the Jew Haym Solomon who helped to finance the War of Independence was an agent of the family, as he died in 1785, before Amschel Rothschild became an international financier.

In 1837 the Rothschilds sent an agent of theirs to establish offices in New York. This was a Jew called Schoenberg, whose name was changed to August Belmont, and who professed Christianity. This Jew had had experience both in the Frankfort and the Naples branches of the Rothschild connection. From 1844 to 1850, Belmont was, through Solomon Rothschild's influence, made the Austrian Consul-General at New York; he then resigned as a protest against Austria's treatment of the Hungarian revolutionary, Kossuth. (It is noted here that Kossuth was a friend of Lord Palmerston). In 1853, Belmont became U.S.A. representative to the Netherlands, living at the Hague for several years. After that, in 1860, he became Chairman of the Democratic National Committee. Altogether it is clear that Belmont had a tremendous power in the United States. He became enormously rich and married the daughter of Commodore Matthew Perry who " opened up " Japan to the western nations.

Meanwhile, the Rothschilds "established offices in the Southern States of the U.S.A. for the purchase of wool, which they shipped to France, where they marketed it . . . . They bought up whole tobacco harvests for supplying the tobacco requirements of the various States. Their own ships carried the enormous cargoes between the United States and France." (A, Vol. II., p. 387).

Thus, when the Civil War (1861-5) broke out between North and South, the Rothschilds of Europe were obviously very deeply involved on both sides. It is important to remember here that they were never in good odour with Napoleon III., who borrowed not from them but from other Jews. Napoleon III. had very definite plans as to the future of America, and the Rothschilds evidently had a somewhat similar scheme. The distrust of Napoleon III. for the Rothschilds, however, made it impossible for them *openly* to support him in his efforts with money.

Napoleon III.'s idea was to establish a new Empire by acquiring Mexico and some of the Southern United States, and he wanted Britain to come in with him to compel the North to abandon the blockade of the Southern ports. The South (the Confederates), hard-pressed, were trying to secure Napoleon III.'s intervention in their favour, which they hoped to get by offering him some territory, viz.: Louisiana and Texas. The Confederate Government had the Jew Judah P. Benjamin as their Secretary of State, and the *Jewish Encyclopædia* (B, Vol. III., p. 30) removes all doubt as to what was going on, for it says : "Unfortunately a thorough study of the diplomacy of the Confederacy has not yet been published, nor any adequate biography of Benjamin, of which that would be the principal chapter. But by such a publication it would be shown how near the Confederacy came to securing European intervention—particularly through the aid of Napoleon III.—by the tempting and statesmanlike efforts of the Confederate State Department under Benjamin's direction, and to the probable transformation of an insurrection into a successful revolution in consequence."

That Benjamin had, before the Civil War, actually conversed with Napoleon at Biarritz on this very subject of a French Dominion in America is revealed in Clew's *Fifty Years in Wall Street* (Z 3, p. 62).

Aided by Jewish loans, through the Credit Mobilier and backed by the Pereira firm, Napoleon's nominee, Maximilian of Austria, landed in

Mexico in 1864 to become its short-lived Emperor. But the plot failed. Britain would not play her part. The man who prevented it was Tsar Alexander II. of Russia! He sent his fleet, such as it was, across the ocean and put it at Abraham Lincoln's disposal, so that the British and French knew that if they attempted to carry out the scheme of Napoleon III., they would find themselves engaged in hostilities with Russia. This bit of secret history has never been allowed to become public property. At the time, the Tsar himself did not advertise it because, immediately afterwards, he was forced by the European situation to make friends with Napoleon III. That the Russian fleet was in American waters at the time, under the command of the Tsar's brother, and was " invited " by Secretary Seward, and that this prevented France and Britain from carrying out their plans is confirmed by Clews (Z 3, p. 59). Clews regarded the presence of the Russian fleet as a lucky incident, but the British and French Governments obviously considered it was deliberate.

Now what did the Rothschilds want ? Their desires may be estimated fairly accurately by quoting the opinion given by Disraeli on the future of America when the Civil War was over :—" It will be an America of armies, of diplomacy, of rival States and manoeuvring Cabinets, of frequent turbulence, and probably of frequent wars." (*Annual Register*, 1863, N.S. cv. 21). Disraeli was Lionel Rothschild's mouth-piece. The Rothschilds wished to reproduce in America the chaotic conditions obtaining in Europe whereby they ruled all States ; a united America would be too powerful for them ; it must be split, and now was the time to do it, but it was awkward that Napoleon III. would not work with them ! What were they to do ? There was only one answer. Support both sides and prevent a win outright for either side, and so force apart the North and the South, with the possibility of the North becoming annexed to Canada. In practice, this meant helping the weak South more than the strong North.

That was what the British Government actually did ; in spite of much liberal sentiment in sympathy with the North, British policy veered round in favour of the South, and the Confederacy was recognised by it and assisted directly by allowing ships to be built, fitted and even manned for it in British ports ; so much so, that, as is well known, Britain had subsequently to pay damages for the activities of the *Alabama* and *Florida* on the high seas.

August Belmont in New York supported the North " with the greatest vigour." " His most valuable service, perhaps, was a constant correspondence with influential friends in Europe, the Rothschilds and others. in which he set forcibly the Northern side in the great conflict." (Z 4, Vol. II., p. 170). The *Encyclopedia Britannica* (R, Vol. III., p. 710) also says that he energetically supported the Union and exerted his influence on financiers in England and France in support of the North. Lionel Rothschild thought that the North would win, says Roth (L).

Meanwhile, the other Rothschilds invested heavily in the bonds of the South and so ultimately of course incurred heavy losses. (B, Vol. X., p. 496).

The Rothschilds, I repeat, backed both sides, their material interests being on both sides, and their political interests requiring a long war and a stalemate, which could only be produced by giving more help to the South than to the North.

Had August Belmont any contacts with Judah P. Benjamin, the Jew who was first Attorney-General, then Secretary for War, and finally Secretary of the Confederate Government ? I find he had. Belmont's wife, a Gentile, had an uncle John Slidell (1793-1871), a partner in the law firm of Slidell, Benjamin & Conrad, in Louisiana, and of which Judah P. Benjamin was also a partner ! This can hardly be a coincidence ; it was obviously Cohen-cidence ! Further, Slidell was one of the two commissaries that the Confederacy sent to France to purchase munitions and arrange for supplies, shipping and other help for the South. Slidell was on familiar terms with Napoleon III. (Z3, p.p. 60-68) and approved of Napoleon's Mexican Adventure. (Z4). His daughter married Baron Frederick Emil D'Erlanger, head of the Jew banking firm in Paris, whose father, Baron Raphael Erlanger of Frankfort had been confidential representative of the Rothschilds. The Erlanger firm financed the Confederates (*Confederate States of America*, by J. C. Schwab, p. 102, New York, 1901) and I have no doubt were assisted by their patrons the Rothschilds, who could do nothing openly because of Napoleon III.'s hearty distrust of them. The Erlangers were also agents for the Credit Mobilier, Rothschilds' rivals.

Abraham Lincoln tried to introduce State Loans to free the people of America from the clutches of the bankers. We need not be surprised therefore that August Belmont " strongly opposed the nomination and election of Lincoln." (Z4, Vol. II.). Lincoln financed the Civil War on state credit, and for that he was murdered in 1865 by the Jewish actor Booth. This Booth was neither a Southerner nor ever owned a slave (*A New American History*, by W. E. Woodward, 1938, p. 475). An attempt to murder Seward was made the same evening ; Seward was the man who gave the invitation to the Russian fleet. An attempt against the Tsar himself was made in Paris in the following year and in 1881 he was blown to pieces by a bomb. Lincoln, Seward and the Tsar were the three people who had chiefly prevented the Jewish partition of the United States !

President Garfield, who held the same views about the true nature of national credit as Lincoln did, was also duly assassinated.

" Lionel Rothschild had a large share in the successful funding of the United States National Debt." (B, Vol. X., p. 501). This would be the Funding Act, 1866, after the Civil War, which retired a large number of greenbacks (State Credit Notes) although the process was suspended within two years.

In 1893, Pierpont Morgan, Belmont and the Rothschilds supplied the U.S.A. Government with three-and-a-half million ozs. of gold in exchange for bonds carrying four per cent. interest and at a price far below the current market price of such securities. This transaction was very unpopular in the States, and with good reason, for the relief offered to the country's finances was only of ten months' duration after which the situation was worse than ever. Then, however, the U.S.A.

Government floated a loan selling its bonds to the public, with gratifying results. (*A History of the American People*, by S. E. Forman, 1922, p. 647).

August Belmont, the Rothschild representative, became Grand Sachem of the Tammany Society which ran Tammany Hall, the centre of boss rule and corruption in New York; this position was extremely useful to the House considering the amount of Rothschild money that was invested in New York. Tammany Hall is a sort of Gentile front for the Jewish Kehilla, or Jewish secret government.

August Belmont died in 1890. His sons, Perry and August, were both prominent in the corrupt politics of the country. Perry Belmont was Chairman of the Committee on Foreign Affairs, 1885-9, and Minister Plenipotentiary to Spain, 1888-9, and held other important posts. The second August Belmont had a son, Morgan Belmont, and through him a grandson, John Mason Belmont; he carried on the firm for the Rothschilds until his death and now Morgan represents the family in it.

CHAPTER VII.

THE ROTHSCHILD GRIP IN OTHER LANDS.

BELGIUM.

THE Rothschilds had great influence with King Leopold (who died in 1865), and, in fact, one of Lionel's sons was named after him (L, p. 35). Karl Rothschild had entertained Leopold in Naples before he came to the Throne; long after, when the latter, as King, thought his Throne was in danger, he deposited five million francs with the Rothschilds to hold for him in case he had to fly the country (A, Vol. II., 274). After that, the Rothschilds were in social relationship with the King.

The Belgian Government obtained the necessary loans for railway construction through the Rothschilds. The affairs of the firm were managed by Baron Leon Lambert who married the daughter of Gustav Rothschild in 1862, and had a son, Henri.

BRAZIL AND SOUTH AMERICA.

So weighed down by Rothschildian loans was Brazil that, since 1825, that country " might have been described as a Rothschild State " (J, p. 9). All loans from 1883 to 1896 were floated by the Rothschilds.

The baneful influences of Rothschild control over Brazil and of debt-control in general in other South American States is at last producing a reaction in those countries.

In Chile, the Rothschilds control nitrates.

At Lima, in Peru, on the opening of the Pan-American Conference in 1939, the city " was festooned with thousands of Swastika flags, and only three American flags were visible " (*Telegraph*, 3rd Jan., 1939).

It is significant that the Presidency of the Latin-American Society has been occupied by Lionel Nathan Rothschild.

EGYPT.

Until the purchase of the Suez Canal shares for the British Government (see p. 20) in 1875, the Rothschilds were not much interested in Egypt.

In 1882, just before the British occupied the country, however, Egypt being almost bankrupt financially, two Jews, Sir H. Drummond Wolff and Sir Henry Goschen went to Egypt to investigate, and as a result, the Rothschilds made a loan of eight-and-a-half million pounds to Egypt, and the British Government guaranteed it; in other words, the Rothschilds "earned" the commission and interest, and the liability was taken by the British tax-payer. The Council of Foreign Bond-holders (see p. 19) was the force which moved the Government in this case. Since then, the Rothschilds have made other loans to Egypt.

PORTUGAL.

The Jew Mendizabel "worked in close alliance with the House of Rothschild which arranged a loan of two million pounds to Portugal in April, 1835." (A, Vol. II., p. 138).

It is impossible, of course, in a small book to cover the whole of the Rothschild money power which exists in all but genuine racial Fascist states; I have dealt with the main items only.

The Rothschild power in Asia is represented by the Sassoon family, in Australia by the Montefiores, whilst their grip on South Africa will be referred to under the heading, Diamonds and Gold (see p. 61).

Since Austria-Hungary was partitioned by the Treaty of Versailles, the Rothschilds, together with Barings and Schroders, and Hambros, have made great loans to its component parts, Austria, Czechoslovakia and Hungary. The effect of this credit made through the four firms, all of alien origin and at least two Jewish, on "British" policy against Hitler will be estimated at its proper value by my readers.

CHAPTER VIII.

THE ROTHSCHILDS AND BRITISH ROYALTY.

ONE of the saddest reflections that Aryan patriots must suffer is in the recognition that Royalty in Europe has gradually succumbed to the influence of the money of the Rothschild family. It is useless to attempt to conceal from one's self the fact that, with few exceptions, the Hereditary Rulers and their families have failed in their duty towards their subjects who look to them for protection from penetrating evils. In many cases, Freemasonry was the agent by which the Kings and Princes were induced to forget why they were Kings and Princes. It is curious to note that Napoleon I., who sprang from ordinary well-born stock, stands out as more Kingly in this respect than Royalties born royal. We must not imagine that Royalty is especially weak because it has encouraged and embraced the Rothschilds when it should have held them at arms' length and made their advances impossible. The fact is that weakness against the power of riches is found in all classes without exception; only a fractional percentage of men and women have the foresight and strength of character to resist and oppose that power, and it is unlikely that such a small community as the Royal Families of Europe would be able to provide many examples of such.

We have seen how the Elector Prince of Hesse-Cassel was gradually induced by his advisers, particularly by Buderus, to trust the Rothschilds in business; we have seen how the Emperor of Austria failed to check his Chancellor Metternich from doing the same under the advice of the Jew von Gentz. That started the rot, and the various Royal Families have since fallen to such an extent that it is of no particular interest to enumerate them.

The shameless effrontery of the Jew knows no bounds, and once a feeling of confidence has been instilled into a princely heart, it is only a matter of insistence, of bribery and gifts to the needy officials and others around the throne, before another barrier is broken down—the social one.

Even in 1809, we find the Royal Dukes, brothers of George IV., doing what common people would then generally refrain from doing. We find the Jew Abraham Goldsmid, the same who helped to finance the French Revolution (see p. 13) acting as host to the Duke of Cambridge, whilst the latter, with the Duke of Cumberland, used to visit Nathan Rothschild in his Piccadilly home. The Prince Regent arranged payments of borrowed money to the Elector of Hesse-Cassel through Nathan's hands.

Queen Victoria long resisted the Rothschild attack. Whatever her faults may have been, she was really Royal and her instincts true. These instincts had to be broken down. First, her advisers had to be penetrated, and Lionel Rothschild wormed his way into friendship with the Prince Consort, to whom he was soon an "adviser." The Queen must have been impressed early in her reign by the Rothschild power in European affairs, for she was then accustomed to send her correspondence to her Uncle Leopold in Belgium by means of the Rothschild courier in preference to the mails or the diplomatic bag. (L, p. 70).

Then, when Disraeli became Prime Minister in 1867, the scheming instrument of the Rothschilds, a Jew, yet not altogether a Jew according to the race-ignorant standards of the time since his head had been damped at an early age, all his cunning and knowledge of the weaker aspects of human nature were brought to bear upon Queen Victoria.

In 1869 we find her still resisting like a Queen. In a letter to Gladstone dated 1st November of that year, in which she referred to a recommendation made to her to promote Lionel Rothschild to the Peerage. she refused in these words :—" It is not only the feeling, of which she cannot divest herself, against making a person of the Jewish religion, a Peer; but she cannot think that one who owes his great wealth to contracts with foreign Governments for Loans, or to successful speculation on the Stock Exchange, can fairly claim a British Peerage. However high Sir L. Rothschild may stand personally in public estimation, this seems to her not less a species of gambling because it is on a gigantic scale and far removed from that legitimate trading which she delights to honour, in which men have raised themselves by patient industry and unswerving probity to positions of wealth and influence."

True protective Royalty spoke there, almost for the last time !

The Queen was horrified at the intimacy of the Prince of Wales (later King Edward VII.) with the Rothschilds ; he had become a close associate of Nathaniel Rothschild when both were students at Trinity College, Cambridge ; and he did not scruple to become an accustomed guest at the magnificent Rothschild country mansions, a practice which he maintained with two generations of that family. In 1878, he was guest at Lord Rosebery's wedding with Hannah Rothschild where Disraeli gave away the bride ; he attended Ferdinand Rothschild's funeral service in a synagogue in 1898. He attended Leopold Rothschild's wedding, also of course at a synagogue. He had the Rothschilds as guests at Sandringham, and was equally familiar with the Jew family of Sassoon at whose houses he partook of hospitality.

At last, the resistance of Queen Victoria was broken down, and Nathaniel became a Baron of England in 1885.

In 1890, although never intimate with a Rothschild, she visited the home of Ferdinand Rothschild at Waddesdon Manor !

When Edward VII. came to the throne, the very first ball he attended with his consort was at 148, Piccadilly, the home of Baron Nathaniel Rothschild. Even Queen Alexandra became a great friend of Nathaniel's wife who was often her hostess.

In 1902, King Edward promoted the Baron to the Privy Council, together with the Jew Sir Ernest Cassel ; this in spite of the strong resistance of Lord Salisbury who resigned his premiership on finding that the King insisted on conferring these Jewish Honours. (*The King and the Imperial Crown*, by Dr. A. B. Keith, p. 105-6, 1936).

It was not merely that Edward liked Jews ; he preferred them. It made his hitherto constricted life easy. Thus from E. F. Benson's *King Edward VII.* :—" Owing to the financial acumen of such friends of his as Baron Hirsch and Mr. Ernest Cassel " (both Jews) " he had no debts at all." Again in *Letters of Prince von Bulow*, translated by F. Whyte, p. 182 (Hutchinson), the German Emperor says of the Jew Beit " He takes care of all the speculations of His Majesty, who must be almost a partner in his transactions. He must always be providing His Majesty with heaps of gold *of which he is always in need. One may say ' he runs the King.' "* (Our italics).

King Edward, when Prince of Wales, borrowed enormous sums from Baron Hirsch on notes of hand ; according to Wm. Le Queux in *Things I Know* (1923, p.p. 26-29) when the Jew died, and the executors wrote Edward for repayment of the sums owing, Lady Hirsch, the widow, burned the notes ; after which he kissed the Jewess's hand !

A man who could sink to that sort of thing would obviously see great advantages in making himself cheap to the Rothschilds, without considering how his familiarity with Jews would react upon his future subjects. King Edward let us all down.

King George V. did not hanker after the society of Jews, but nevertheless it cannot be said that he caused any reaction to set in against their recognition.

The Duke of Windsor followed in his grandfather's footsteps, and it is probable that his downfall was due to his Jewish *entourage*. He would visit Rothschild homes both in England and abroad, and after the people of England had turned him down, he took refuge at once in Rothschild castles in Austria, and Baron and Baroness Eugene Rothschild were guests at his wedding to Mrs. Simpson. The married pair seem to prefer Jews as companions.

The present King George VI. also favours Jews, and the Queen's niece on her marriage actually received a present of a Rothschild cheque. When the Duke and Duchess of Gloucester met the " exiled " Duke of Windsor in Paris in November in 1938, they all had tea at Baron de Rothschild's.

It is of course no accident that most of the male members of the British Royal Family who have forgotten their Royal Duty by mixing socially with Jews have been Grand Masters in Freemasonry; whilst those who have not shown a preference for Jewish company have not been Masons.

CHAPTER IX.

GENTILE INTERMARRIAGES WITH THE ROTHSCHILDS.

IN Britain, the first to fall for a Rothschild was *Hon. Henry Fitzroy* who married Hannah Rothschild, daughter of Nathan Mayer, in 1839. He was the second son of the second Baron Southampton. It is interesting to note that an uncle of his, Hon. Warren Fitzroy, had set the degenerate example by marrying a Jewess as long ago as 1794. Fitzroy's Rothschild wife became a " Christian." He himself in later life became an intimate friend of Lord Palmerston.

He died in 1859, leaving a half-caste daughter who married Sir Coutts Lindsay, Bart., in 1864, and had two daughters; one of these married Rev. T. S. Henrey of Old Brentford, and the other remained unmarried. The Rothschild blood has here died out.

In 1873, another member of the British aristocracy forgot his race and duty; this was *Hon. Eliot Yorke*, son of 4th Earl of Hardwicke, who married one of the daughters of Sir Anthony Rothschild, Bart. In this case, the bride remained a Jewess by religion. Although an M.P., her husband took little active part in politics, and died, fortunately without issue.

Four years after this marriage, the other daughter of Sir Anthony Rothschild, Bart., followed her sister's example by marrying a Gentile, *Mr. Cyril Flower*, whilst retaining her Jewish religion. Flower became a prominent Liberal politician, and was made by Gladstone a junior Lord of the Treasury in 1866. He became *Lord Battersea* in 1892. Once again, Providence defended England, and there were no children of the marriage. It was Flower who befriended Asquith and " took the greatest pleasure in offering him all the opportunities that lay in his power of meeting such men as would appreciate him and be useful to him in his career." (W, p. 268).

A letter to Cyril Flower from Sir Dighton Probyn is quoted congratulating him on his marriage to the Jewess in these words:—"You are marrying a person fit to be the Queen of England." (M, p.p. 170-1). As Sir Dighton Probyn was Comptroller and Treasurer of the Royal Household, and was later Private Secretary to King Edward VII., and a V.C. into the bargain, one may judge the kind of atmosphere in which that Household was developing.

In 1878, the Rothschilds scored two bulls-eyes, marrying into two of the aristocratic families of France and England, respectively.

Marguerite Rothschild, daughter of Mayer Karl, and granddaughter of Karl Rothschild of Naples became the wife of Agenor, Duc de Gramont, Prince de Bidache, as his second wife. They have children and grandchildren.

In the same year, the 5th Lord Rosebery married Hannah, only daughter of Mayer Amschel Rothschild, son of Nathan Mayer, the bride being " given away " at the ceremony by Disraeli. She " made Lansdowne House the focus of social Liberalism and was an important element in the organisation of the Liberal Party." (B, Vol. X., p. 472). She remained a Jewess by religion. Her husband was Under-Secretary for the Home Office, 1881-3; Lord Privy Seal and First Commissioner of Works, 1885; Foreign Secretary in 1886, and again 1892-4; and Prime Minister, 1894-5.

That he acted throughout for the Rothschild interest is indicated by the fact that as Prime Minister he discussed with Rhodes the possibilities of overcoming President Kruger by a filibustering raid (see p. 62) with the object of securing the Jewish mining interests, of which Rothschilds represented the main share, under a subservient " British" regime.

Lord Rosebery's two sons were the present Lord Rosebery (6th) and Right Hon. Neil Primrose. His two daughters married respectively Sir C. J. C. Grant, actually grandson of Sir Robert Grant who was knighted for his attempts in Parliament to emancipate the Jews, and the first Marquess of Crewe. Neil Primrose's daughter brought Rothschild blood into Lord Halifax's family, she marrying the latter's son and heir. The present Lord Rosebery, a half-caste Jew, has surviving issue (1) a daughter who married H. A. Vivian Smith of the Quaker family, and (2) Neil Archibald Primrose, heir to the title.

The surviving child of the Marquess of Crewe by his Jewish wife is the wife of 9th Duke of Roxburghe. Thus through this disastrous Rosebery-Rothschild union, no less than four titled families of British nobility are contaminated by Jewish blood.

It will be noted that the half-Rothschild, Rt. Hon. Neil Primrose was Foreign Under-Secretary, 1915, and Joint Parliamentary Secretary to the Treasury, 1916-17. This half-Jew married the daughter of 17th Earl of Derby; her brother is Oliver Stanley, the new 1940 War Minister who replaced the Jew Hore-Belisha.

Thus, in the War Cabinet, both the Foreign Secretary Lord Halifax, and the War Minister, Mr. Oliver Stanley, have close family connections with the Rothschilds, which, considering that the war is being fought

46

for the Jews and for no other reason at all, must, I suppose, be considered an appropriate arrangement.

Barthe Marie Rothschild, sister of the Rothschildian Duchess of Gramont, married Alexandre, Prince de Wagram, in 1882 ; but it is not absolutely certain that the latter's family was pure Gentile in blood. They had issue.

In 1934, Rosemary Rothschild, daughter of Lionel Nathan, and granddaughter of Leopold Rothschild, married Hon. Denis Berry, second son of Lord Kemsley, of the newspaper-owning Berry family. The significance of this union is apparently not appreciated by Lord Camrose, Lord Kemsley's brother, for in 1939 he published a booklet purporting to show that there was little or no Jew-control or Jew-interest in the London Press. The Berry family controls Allied Newspapers, Ltd., including *The Telegraph, Sunday Times, Financial Times*, and many leading provincial dailies.

The third Baron (British title) Rothschild took to wife a daughter of Mr. St. John Hutchinson, who until then was Sir Oswald Mosley's favourite counsel.

Adrien Thierry of the French Diplomatic Service, Ambassador in Bucharest, 1939, is married to the daughter of Henri Rothschild.

CHAPTER X.

GENTILE FRIENDS OF THE ROTHSCHILDS.

THE Rothschild family cunningly and perseveringly insinuated itself into " society " and particularly into relationships with politicians who wielded power in the affairs of Europe. It would of course be impossible to indicate more than a few of the most important of these " friendships," together with some of less importance which, however, may be of special interest to my readers.

Lord Palmerston. 1784-1865.

Prime Minister, 1855 ; many times Foreign Secretary. Described in *Occult Theocracy*, Vol. I., p. 264 (Lady Queenborough) as the " patriarch of European Freemasonry." Intimate friend of Kossuth and Mazzini ; supporter of the 1848 French Revolution ; influenced Napoleon III. to appoint Prince Murat, Grand Master of the Grand Orient Masons, as King of Naples ; enemy of Russia, and prevented Austria from joining Russia in the Crimean War, thus ensuring Russia's defeat. Censored by Queen Victoria for forming important decisions without consulting her.

In a letter written by H. Reeve to Chas. Greville, he states " Rothschild says : ' Lord Palmerston is a friend of the House ; he dines with us at Frankfort, but he has the disadvantage of depressing the funds all over Europe without giving us notice.' " (X, letter 20th December, 1845).

The Jewish Encyclopedia (B, Vol. IX., p. 454) writes of the Jew Don Pacifico who lived in Athens, " When the Easter burning of Judas Iscariot customary in that city was given up in 1847 at the request of the Rothschilds, the mob in revenge burned down Pacifico's house, whereupon he claimed compensation to the amount of £26,618. When this rather preposterous claim . . . . was not treated seriously by the Greek Government, Lord Palmerston sent a British fleet to Piraeus (1850) and seized all the ships in the harbour." This led to the withdrawal of the French Ambassador from London. As a consequence of all this, the Government was defeated by 37 votes, but in spite of that the Cabinet decided to do nothing about it. In the debate, " Such shuffling, special pleading, and paltry evasions were never before heard from public men of their eminence and character " (K, 19th May, 1850).

It is likely that Lord Palmerston used the Rothschilds at least as much as they used him. He was a friend of Hon. Henry Fitzroy whose wife was a Rothschild, and he spoke in 1840 at the Mansion House meeting of protest against the threatened execution of the Jewish Ritual Murderers of Damascus (see p. 53).

Lord Macaulay. 1800-1859.

This impecunious historian became an M.P. for a pocket borough and in 1833 for Leeds. In the latter year he was the principal supporter of Sir R. Grant when the latter successfully steered a Bill for Jewish emancipation through the House of Commons (but it was stopped in the Lords). Presumably for this service to the Jews, Macaulay obtained within a year a seat on the Supreme Council of India, *with a salary of £10,000*. His chief works were written subsequent to this period and we may be sure they would not err on the side of "anti-semitism."

In 1839 he became Secretary for War, and that was the first year of the Afghan War ; he remained in office for nearly two years.

He was a favourite guest of Nathaniel Rothschild.

J. T. Delane. 1817-79.

Delane was Editor of *The Times*, 1841-77. He was a personal friend of Lord Palmerston, who has already been dealt with (see p. 47).

Delane was intimate with the Rothschild family and a constant and welcome visitor to their houses ; so intimate indeed, that (quoting from *The Times*, 23rd Nov., 1926) the two daughters of Sir Anthony Rothschild often rode with Delane in Rotten Row, as well as in Buckinghamshire, "and he took a kindly interest in their lessons." He was described by Lady Battersea (Constance Rothschild) as "a dear friend." (Her *Reminiscences*, p. 106). He was a frequent guest both of Mayer and of Lionel Rothschild ; it was at the latter's house that he first met Disraeli in 1863, and he was present at the wedding of Alphonse.

Delane was Editor of *The Times* before he met the Rothschilds, but in 1847 (26th Jan.) his diary shows that he " sat up late and went to Mayer Rothschild's house in Piccadilly to assist him in preparing his address " (election address, and Mayer was duly returned).

A. I. Dasent, in his *John Delane*, 1908, Vol. II., p. 341, gives the whole thing away :—" For eleven years Delane fought for him (Lionel Rothschild) the battle for the admission of the Jews to Parliament."

In the section on the Press, specific instances are given as to Rothschild influence over *Times* policy.

W. E. Gladstone. 1809-98.

Gladstone did not fall for the Rothschilds in early life. As in the case of Queen Victoria, they literally wore him down. He strongly supported Jewish emancipation in 1847, having previously been opposed to it.

His social acquaintance with the Rothschilds began in the late fifties, when he used to visit Lionel Rothschild at his Piccadilly home (W, p. 239), where he was also a frequent guest of Nathaniel after Lionel's decease. Nathaniel was then professing to be a Unionist, and his was the only Unionist house in London at which the Gladstones were wont to dine. Gladstone was intimate with the two daughters of Sir Anthony Rothschild, whom he first met about 1879 ; by 1888 he was calling Mrs. Flower by her first name, and in 1889 got so far as to go on a cruise on Mrs. Yorke's yacht. Gladstone tried to induce Queen Victoria to make Lionel a Peer in 1869 but failed ; he succeeded however in 1885 in getting Nathaniel made a Baron of England.

What with Disraeli and Gladstone both in their hands, Rothschild policy was easy to enforce upon a British Government.

Sir Bernard Eric Barrington. 1847-1918.

Whilst attending the Berlin Congress (1878) he was writing intimately on politics to the Rothschild, Mrs. Flower (M, p. 148). He was précis writer to the Foreign Secretary. Later he became Private Secretary to Lord Salisbury. In 1906 he was Assistant Under-Secretary for Foreign Affairs.

Viscount Morley. 1838-1923.

Was Secretary of State for India, 1905-10, and Lord President of Council, 1910-14. Before that, ardent supporter of Gladstone.

From about 1890, " the happiest days of his life were passed " at the home of Lord Battersea. (W, p. 173). On one occasion in 1892, Morley accepted free quarters and coals from Cyril Flower, but in thanking him for this he writes : " but I cry out for Mrs. Flower and Lady de Rothschild."

Morley was also a guest at Tring Park, Baron Nathaniel's country seat.

Rt. Hon. Augustine Birrell. 1850-1933.

He was Chief Secretary to the Lord Lieutenant of Ireland, 1907-16, and was made scapegoat for the deplorable exhibition of slackness and sluggishness which left lawlessness unchecked and fomented the Rebellion of 1916 ; his Assistant Secretary was the Jew Sir M. Nathan.

From 1890, Birrell was an intimate of Lord Battersea and his Rothschild wife.

Rt. Hon. H. H. *Asquith.* 1852-1928. *Earl of Oxford.*

Asquith was Prime Minister 1908-16, and Secretary for War, 1914.
It was Cyril Flower, husband of a Rothschild, who helped to push

Asquith forward into influential circles. (W, p. 268). He attended Asquith's second wedding (to Margot Tennant).

In 1892, Lady Anthony Rothschild had Asquith's five children to stay at her residence for Christmas ! (M, p. 224).

Asquith was an occasional guest at Tring Park, Nathaniel Rothschild's seat and " at one period, Alfred Rothschild used to go to 10, Downing Street every morning to see Asquith, another close friend, who set great store on his advice." (L, p. 159).

In Asquith's *Memoirs and Reflections*, he speaks of " our friends Jimmy and Dolly," referring in these intimate terms to James Rothschild and his wife. Lady Oxford (née Margot Tennant) writes of her " week-end visits " to the Rothschilds and of her " dear friend,' Alice Sassoon. (Y, p.p. 84 and 124).

Rt. Hon. A. J. Balfour. 1848-1930.

Offered Palestine as a National Home for the Jews in 1917, as the price for getting the United States of America into the War.

He was a regular visitor at Baron Nathaniel Rothschild's Ascot house. (L, p. 229). He was himself host to Lady Battersea in 1911. His brother Gerald was described by the latter as " a close friend of my husband and myself."

Cecil Rhodes. 1853-1902.

His connection with the Rothschilds is dealt with under the section " Diamonds and Gold " (see p. 61).

A. B. Freeman-Mitford, later 1st Lord Redesdale. 1837-1916.

He was in the Diplomatic Corps at St. Petersburg, Pekin and Tokyo, and when he came home in 1873 he was one of Lionel Rothschild's weekly visitors.

Lady Snowden. 1881 . . . Wife of Sir Philip Snowden.

Sir Philip Snowden was " Labour " Chancellor of Exchequer, 1924 and 1929-31.

At a Jewish charity meeting in London on 19th March, 1935, Lady Snowden said " For over fourteen years she had counted Lady Rothschild as her best friend " (this was Nathaniel's wife).

Viscount Haldane. 1856-1928.

Secretary of State for War, 1905-12 ; Lord High Chancellor, 1912-15.

In Lord Haldane's autobiography, he says :—" I was also very intimate with the Rothschild family. At Tring Park, I had a room which was always reserved for me, and I paid week-end visits to Lord and Lady Rothschild with great regularity. With them both I was very intimate. Towards the end of his life, in 1915, I was in temporary charge of the Foreign Office while my colleague Grey was on holiday. It was ascertained that a steamer had sailed from South America, and that, although neutral, there was reason to believe that she contained supplies intended for the Germans. There was no material to act on, and the only way was to use private influence. I motored to Lord Rothschild's house in Piccadilly, and found him lying down. . . . . But he stretched out his hand before I could speak and said 'Haldane, I do not know what you have come for, except to see me, but I have said to myself that if Haldane asks me to write a cheque for £25,000 and ask no questions, I will do it on the spot.' I told him it was not for a cheque, but only to get a ship stopped that I was come. He sent a message to stop the ship at once. I knew his brothers and other members of the Rothschild family also very well, and used to stay at their houses and dine with them very much. My friendship extended to the Paris Branch of the family, and to Princess Wagram and Baroness James de Rothschild, Lady Rothschild's sisters. Every year I used to go to the Chateau Gros Bois near Paris to spend a week-end before Christmas with Prince and Princess Wagram."

The most remarkable thing about the above extract is its candour.

Lord Kitchener. 1850-1916.

Lord Kitchener was "on terms of the deepest intimacy" with Alfred Rothschild from the time of Kitchener's first Egyptian years. (L, p. 158). He received valuable presents from this Rothschild. (L, p. 242).

General Ludendorff said of Kitchener, in a letter on view in the United Services Museum in Whitehall :—

"His mysterious death was the work neither of a German mine nor of a German torpedo, but of that power which would not permit the Russian Army to recover with the help of Lord Kitchener because the destruction of Czarist Russia had been determined upon. Lord Kitchener's death was caused by his abilities."

The following is an extract from *The Diary of Lord Bertie*, 1914-18 (P, Vol. I., p. 134) :—" The Dardanelles expedition was known only to the Inner Ring ; Louis Mallet heard of it at a dinner from Leo de Rothschild, who had learned it from Alfred de Rothschild, who may have picked up the information in the course of his daily visits to Kitchener at the War Office and 10, Downing Street. There is no such thing as a secret nowadays."

Nor would anyone expect secrecy under such circumstances !

At the Dardanelles, the Turks were ready for us, and we lost thousands and thousands of our best men, and the chief object of the expedition to boot.

Lady Cynthia Mosley. 1898-1933.

This was the first wife of Sir Oswald Mosley, and granddaughter of Levi Leiter of Chicago. She died 1933.

At her memorial service, among the numerous Jews present were Mr. James de Rothschild, Emil Cohn, Lady Melchett (representing Lord Melchett), Mrs. Edward Cahan and Mr. Beddington-Behrens (*Times*, 20th May, 1933).

Rt. Hon. Sir Auckland Geddes. 1879 . . .

Chairman of two Rothschild companies, viz. :—(1) Rio Tinto Co., Ltd., the Spanish copper mines (see p. 58) and (2) Rhokana Corporation, Ltd., the Rhodesian copper mines ; the debentures of both these companies are secured by trust deeds dated 1931, to L. N. and A. G. Rothschild.

Sir Auckland Geddes was Ambassador to the U.S.A. 1920-24.

His brother, Sir Eric Geddes has held innumerable key appointments.

Count Ciano, Fascist Foreign Minister in Italy. 1903- . . .

Count Ciano was a friend of the Rothschilds and stayed with them when he came over to this country on a political visit.

His father, Admiral Constanzo Ciano, is stated in Rabbi S. S. Wise's paper *Public Opinion*, Nov., 1939, p. 6, to have married a Jewess ; this statement was made in an article by a Jewess, Gina Lombroso. Italian anti-Jewism is rather an anæmic affair, as the Fascist Government contains several members of Jewish blood.

Anthony Eden, Minister for Dominions, 1939.

This politician, like his war-mongering colleagues, Winston Churchill and Duff Cooper has many friends among the Jews.

Eden used to sit next the Rothschilds at public dinners, and his seat, or rather the one reserved for him, at the Jubilee Procession of George V. was also next the Rothschilds.

" Eden and Philip Sassoon are close friends, They share a love of pictures, and oriental poetry. In London, they sup together several times a week," *Cavalcade*, 18th April, 1936.

Sir Philip Sassoon's mother was a Rothschild.

" Eden and Sassoon have been friends for years " said the *News Review*, 21st July, 1938, in discussing the fact that Sir Philip Sassoon had become involved in controversy with Mr. Chamberlain. " Mr. Chamberlain discovered that Sir Philip had been allowing Anthony Eden and his satellites to hold meetings in his room at the House of Commons."

When Anthony Eden flew back from Geneva via Paris in August, 1935, after the League of Nations had been discussing Italy's attack on Abyssinia, he landed at Hythe to visit first his friend Sassoon.

" The voice that breathed o'er Eden " evidently spoke Yiddish.

Commander Oliver Locker-Lampson. 1881 . . . .

This fanatical Jew-lover, whose antics with a shot-gun during Professor Einstein's visit to this country as a refugee so amused the anti-Jewish world, has been from childhood a friend of the Rothschilds, particularly of Lady Battersea.

It may be remembered that the Commander was Russian Representative of the Ministry of Information in 1918, just after the Bolshevik Revolution. His " Hands off Britain " campaign against the Soviets (which had confiscated the Rothschild oil wells at Baku) never once mentioned that Bolshevism was Jewish. Who financed that movement ? When the movement collapsed in 1933, the Commander advertised that he had £960 worth of badges, sleeve-links, hat-clips and gramophone records, collectively described as Loyalist Emblems, to dispose of !

In 1933, the Commander brought in a Bill " to promote and

extend opportunities of citizenship for Jews resident outside the British Empire."

In 1936, when the Government decided to prosecute the author of this book for speaking the truth about the Jews, it was Locker-Lampson who was chosen to be the official spokesman in Parliament to bring the frightful crime to its notice.

The Quaker families of *Gurney*, *Pease* and *Buxton* have always been on very friendly terms with the Rothschilds.

CHAPTER XI.

ROTHSCHILD FAMILY RELATIONSHIPS WITH OTHER JEWS.

THE MONTEFIORE FAMILY.

THE Rothschilds were related by marriage to the Sephardic Jewish family of Montefiore as follows :—

Abraham Montefiore, brother of Sir Moses, married Jeanette, daughter of the senior Amschel Mayer Rothschild in 1815.

Nathan Mayer Rothschild, of London, Amschel's son, married the sister-in-law of Sir Moses Montefiore in 1806.

Abraham Montefiore's daughter, Louisa, married Sir Anthony Rothschild, Bart., in 1840.

The Montefiores themselves linked up with the big financial Jews Goldsmid by the marriage in 1850 of Abraham Montefiore's son, Nathaniel, to the daughter of Sir I. L. Goldsmid, Bart.

Sir Moses Montefiore, Bart. (1784-1885), after 1812 until his death "lived in New Court, close to his friend Rothschild ; and the brothers Montefiore, as the brokers of that financial genius, became wealthy men." Thus says the *Jewish Encyclopedia* (B, Vol. VIII., p. 668), so there can hardly be any argument that Sir Moses Montefiore depended on and represented the Rothschild interest.

Thus, in 1824, together with Rothschild, he helped to found the Alliance Insurance Company as a sort of Jew-controlled rival to Lloyds.

We may take it that the rivalry between the Goldsmid firm and that of the Rothschilds was ended by the Montefiore-Goldsmid marriage mentioned above.

It is notable that Sir Moses Montefiore's son Leonard was a very intimate friend of Lord Milner and Arnold Toynbee.

It was Sir Moses Montefiore who was sent out to Egypt and Constantinople after the Jewish Ritual Murders at Rhodes and Damascus (U, p.p. 23 seq.) to bribe the Khedive and the Sultan into hushing up this Jewish practice, after the failure of the Austrian House of Rothschild to achieve this object through the Austrian Consulates, Austria being in need of loans from the House. Referring to the Rhodes murder, the *Jewish Encyclopedia* states : " owing to the efforts of Count Camondo, Cremieux and Montefiore, a firman was obtained from the Sultan which declared all accusations of ritual murder null and void." The cost of this firman is not stated, but the reader will note with interest that the Paris Rothschild agent Cremieux reinforced the endeavours of Montefiore, their London broker. Camondo was banker to the Ottoman Government, and a Jew.

Writing of the Damascus case, the converted Rabbi Chevalier P. L. B, Drach states in his *Harmony between the Church and the Synagogue* (1844, Paris, p. 79) "Money played a great role in this business."

Another member of the Montefiore expedition was Salomon Munk, who had previously been teacher to the Paris Rothschild family, his pupils being Alphonse and Gustav.

The results of these bare-faced briberies have been completely misrepresented in the Jew-controlled "British" Press. Thus, the Damascus prisoners were released but not exonerated, whilst the Sultan's firman was the merest sophistry; but for further details see my other book (reference U).

It is particularly interesting that Pope Pius IX. refused to give an audience to Sir Moses Montefiore on his way back from this exploit, although the Jew persisted in his efforts to see His Holiness with typical shameless effrontery.

The Montefiores are the Jewish Kings of Australia : the first to go there was Jacob (1801-95) who arrived in South Australia in 1843 as agent for the Rothschilds (B, Vol. VIII., p. 666) where his reception by the Governor and the people is described as "enthusiastic."

THE WORMS FAMILY.

Baron Solomon Benedict de Worms, father of Lord Pirbright, lived in Nathan Rothschild's house in London as a boy ; Nathan's sister was the boy's mother.

The estates of the Worms family in Ceylon were known as the Rothschild estates. Baron Pirbright, a "Conservative" politician, was more than once Parliamentary Secretary to the Board of Trade, and from 1888 to 1892 became Under-Secretary for the Colonies.

THE SAMUELS.

As stated on p. 59, the Samuel family was financed by the Rothschilds from the nineties of the last century, when the first Viscount Bearsted began to interest himself in the sea-transport of oil.

THE SASSOON FAMILY.

This family of Baghdad Jews is related by marriage to the Rothschilds. It represents the Rothschild power in India and China.

Sir E. A. Sassoon, Bart., married the daughter of Baron Gustave de Rothschild in 1887, and had two children, Sir Philip Sassoon and the Marchioness of Cholmondeley. Lady Sassoon was a member of the "Souls," the notorious gang of which Balfour and Margot Tennant were members.

Leopold Rothschild married a Perugia, sister of Mrs. Arthur Sassoon.

As stated elsewhere, Sir Philip Sassoon was the bosom friend of the war-mongering politician Anthony Eden. Sir Philip was Field-Marshal Haig's Private Secretary throughout the Great War ; Private Secretary to Lloyd George at the Peace Conference; and was "British" representative at the League of Nations discussion in 1933 as to the possibilities of forming an International Air-Force. He was a constant associate of the Duke of Windsor when the latter was Prince of Wales.

King Edward VII. became familiar with the Sassoon family, setting the bad example to his grandson. He was a wedding-guest at the Rothschild-Sassoon marriage.

THE FRANKLIN FAMILY.

This family of banking Jews has long had relations with the Rothschilds. Jacob Franklin (1809-1877) was Secretary to the North of France Railway and other French railways and became auditor of the chief Brazilian railways. All these concerns were under Rothschild control. His nephew, Frederic Samuel Franklin had two daughters who married Sassoons.

CHAPTER XII.

ROTHSCHILDS AND PRESS CONTROL.

THE power of the Rothschilds to influence public opinion by means of press control has been too often acknowledged and exercised for any doubt to remain on the matter. A newspaper has to pay its way, and is, except in the rare cases where its editor or owner is a man of unusual character, particularly susceptible to the favours which Jews of unlimited means can bestow upon it, to say nothing of the detrimental effects those same unlimited means can produce if applied in a hostile manner.

The Jew poet Bialik, in an address given to Jews at the Jewish University in Jerusalem on 11th May, 1933, said :—" Not in vain have Jews been drawn to journalism. In their hands it became a mighty weapon highly fitted to meet their needs in their war of survival·"

Note these words " weapon " and " war."

It is ridiculous then, considering that the Rothschilds have throughout the 19th century been the most powerful Jewish financiers in Europe, to suppose that they have not been the principal controllers of the Press for the purpose which Bialik so accurately defines.

When, therefore, *The Graphic* of 26th July, 1879, stated that " the Press of the Continent is to a large extent in the hands of Jews," it is equivalent to saying it was largely in the hands of Rothschilds.

The whole subject of Press Control in Britain by Jews is dealt with in a special pamphlet issued by the Imperial Fascist League called *Jewish Press Control.* I must confine myself to some known examples of what must have been the general practice for over 100 years.

Most noteworthy is the extreme intimacy of Mr. J. T. Delane, Editor of *The Times* between 1841 to 1877, with the Rothschilds, as already described (see p. 48).

We know that Sir Moses Montefiore introduced the Jew Samuel

Phillips to the staff of *The Times* where he became Chief Literary Editor, professing Christianity, his son becoming Private Secretary to the Archbishop of Canterbury, Dr. Benson! We know that this Phillips tried to influence the provincial press not to pin Lord Derby down to a pledge of protection in 1852. We know that in 1872, on the last to day of the year, the Russian Ambassador in London, Brunnow, wrote the Russian Chancellor saying that he was persuading Lionel Rothschild to use his influence on *The Times* to adopt a policy of peace and conciliation, and that Brunnow had used the same influence in 1863. (*Cambridge Historical Journal*, I, No. I, 1923). We know that the Rothschilds had been urged by a Cabinet Minister to bring pressure on *The Times* to induce it to modify its hostile attitude towards Germany during the Boer War in 1900; this was of course long after Delane's decease. (A, Vol. II., p. 453). The Rothschilds could do what no Cabinet Minister could achieve!

We know that Lord Kemsley's son Denis has married a Rothschild and that Lord Kemsley and his brother Lord Camrose are Press Kings.

We know that *The Standard* had to close down at the outbreak of the Great War, 1914-18, because the Austrian Embassy "which had been surreptitiously financing it, could no longer make payments" (speech in House of Commons, 21st Nov., 1938, by Rt. Hon. T. Johnston, M.P.). Who ruled Austria, the Hapsburgs or the Rothschilds?

We know that the Rothschilds are chief shareholders in *The Economist*.

We know that Alfred Rothschild gave *The Evening Times* a gift of £1,000 to enable it to carry on. (L, p. 148).

It is the same all over the Continent where "democracy" prevails. The Rothschilds control the *Agence Havas*, *Le Temps* and *La Revue de Paris*, and, until Hitler took over Austria, the *Neue Freie Presse* of Vienna.

The most striking instances in which the Rothschild money-control of newspapers has been exercised have been in the deliberate suppression of news about Jewish Ritual Murders, and the vilification and abuse of prosecuting counsel and judges in such cases. Thus, the influence was brought to bear on the Damascus murder, 1840: the Tisza Eszlar case, 1882; the Polna case, 1899; and the Kiev case, 1911.

CHAPTER XIII.

ROTHSCHILD CONTROL OF RAW MATERIALS.

MERCURY.

THAT the Rothschilds controlled Mercury is a fact which cannot be denied in the face of the statement to that effect in the *Jewish Encyclopædia* (B., Vol. V, p. 384).

Nathan Rothschild sent Lionel to Madrid and the latter obtained the lease of the Almaden mines in Spain in 1832, and received the Order of Isabella the Catholic from the Queen Regent of that country! This mining concession was obtained by the House of Rothschild in consideration of a loan of 15 million francs to the Spanish Government at a low rate of interest. In a few years, the income from these mines was anything between 1¼ million to 2 million francs. Thus the Quicksilver monopoly was established, the Vienna House having previously purchased the Austrian mines of Idria. The Rothschilds doubled the price of mercury, and their monopoly lasted until 1863 by which time Mercury was discovered in the United States of America.

In the years 1835 to 1837, the Rothschilds were in a somewhat desperate position because of these quicksilver interests in Spain. Don Carlos was fighting to gain the throne from the Queen Regent and was threatening the safety of the Almaden mines. The Rothschilds, whose agent in Madrid, the Jew Mendizabal was the Queen Regent's Finance Minister, supported the Queen Regent, but were hampered by the facts that they had little faith in Spain's credit and that their Austrian patron, the Chancellor Metternich, strongly favoured the cause of Don Carlos. The Rothschilds therefore actually " made great efforts to secure the armed intervention of England and France " and were successful in that the French lent the Queen Regent the services of the Foreign Legion, whilst Britain raised a volunteer force which was financed by Nathan Rothschild. (A, Vol. II, p. 124). As in 1940, the French and British were sent to fight the Jews' battles. At last, to please Metternich, the Rothschilds pretended that the Spanish Government had been guilty of bad faith, and they " beared " the Spanish funds in Paris and London bringing them down from 70 to 37. In spite of all this, Don Carlos's inadequacy led to his defeat in the field, and the Rothschild mines were safe again.

NICKEL.

The principal supplies of Nickel, used for hardening purposes in steel manufacture, and for which there is no known substitute, were in Canada, New Caledonia and Norway. The Canadian supplies are controlled by the Jew Lord Melchett, and the New Caledonian mines by the Paris Rothschilds.

What this means exactly is exemplified by a curious occurrence in the Great War 1914-18. Nickel had been declared contraband by the British who cut off Germany's supplies from Canada. However, on 1st October, 1914, a Norwegian steamer loaded with 2,500 tons of the metal from New Caledonia and consigned to Krupp in Germany was stopped by the French Navy and taken to Brest as a prize of war. Immediately an order came from Paris to release the ship, which was then allowed to proceed to Hamburg ! The French did not declare nickel to be contraband until May, 1915, by which time Germany had made sure of her supplies, supplementing them by bringing over from America a further 400 tons in the submarine *Deutschland*; this nickel must have been purchased in the United States from New Caledonia by arrangement (Z, pp. 166-7).

Who made the arrangement ?

Who ordered the Norwegian steamer at Brest to be released ?

One guess will suffice as an answer to both questions.

The French Rothschild Company was called Le Nickel, and had on its Board of Directors two Germans closely associated with Krupp and with the *Metallgesellschaft* of Frankfort, of which the Kaiser was a large shareholder.

That is what Rothschild control signified.

Since then, Finland promises to be the future chief source of Nickel, and the potentialities of the new mines in the arctic region of Petsamo in that country are enormous. These mines are owned by the Jew Lord Melchett's International Nickel Co. of Canada. Their existence will no doubt influence the amount of actual help to Finland which will be rendered by Britain against the Soviets' cowardly attack, but the intelligent reader will not allow himself to lose sympathy with the gallant Finns on that account.

COPPER.

From the beginning of this century, the Rothschilds have had an important share in the Rio Tinto Mines in southern Spain, and the Trust Deed (dated 1931) for the Company's Debentures is in favour of L.N. & A. G. Rothschild. These mines also produce Sulphur ; Rear-Admiral Consett in his *Triumph of Unarmed Forces* (1923), p. 228, shows how the Rio Tinto Company during the World War 1914-18 sent to Denmark enormous amounts of pyrites containing sulphur for the purpose of mixing with raw phosphatic materials from North Africa to make fertiliser, obviously for German use.

According to the *Jewish Encyclopædia* (B, Vol. V, p. 384) the world control of Copper was (in 1903) in the hands of the Jew firms Lewisohn Bros. & Guggenheim Sons.

LEAD.

Among the most important Lead-mines in the world are those of the Spanish Company Societe Miniere de Penarroya which produces one-eighth of the world's total. Since 1883, the Paris Rothschilds controlled the Company and in 1909 they allied themselves with the Frankfort *Metallgesellschaft* (which meant Krupp and the Kaiser, as stated previously in this Chapter). This arrangement continued until 31st December, 1916, and must have been most profitable for Rothschild Freres during the first two years of the war, when they sent 150,000 tons to Germany, via Switzerland. (Z, p. 167).

OIL.

The story of Rothschild Oil-interests can be largely told by means of extracts from well-authenticated sources.

" The house of Rothschild, and more especially its Paris Branch, had been strongly interested in the Caucasian petroleum industry ever since 1883. Here it controlled two important companies, the Caspian-Black Sea Company, and, since 1898, the Mazut Company . . . these Rothschild companies had had to fight hard against the overwhelming superiority of Standard Oil. Thus it was only natural that the capitalists who owned them should strive to strengthen and expand their influence in the oil industry by giving financial support to the Dutch Company." (Z. 1, p. 47).

The *Jewish Encyclopædia* (B, Vol. X, p. 496), says that the interest of the Rothschilds in the Baku Oil-wells made them the chief competitor of Standard Oil Company.

In a letter dated 14th March 1901, Sir Cecil Spring-Rice wrote of "Baku, an enormous town in a desert, breeding petroleum, once the home and temple of fire-worshippers—now mostly owned by the Rothschilds." (D, Vol. I, p. 338).

Then appears Deterding on the scene, an official of the Royal Dutch Company, later to become Sir Henri Deterding ; this man is described by W. Thompson in an article " World Oil-War or Entente," published in *Asia*, May 1923, pp. 236-8, as " a Jew by race " ; whilst the *News of the World*, 5th February, 1939, said he was " of Jewish descent."

" It was Deterding who induced the House of Rothschild to give Royal Dutch its backing, which undoubtedly saved the Company from ruin." (Z. 1, p. 48).

The Jew Marcus Samuel " built an experimental oil-tanker with money borrowed from the Rothschilds of Paris." (Z. 2, p. 21).

The Royal Dutch Company allied itself with the Shell Transport of Marcus Samuel (afterwards Viscount Bearsted), in 1897, and later, in 1902 with a sales firm, the Asiatic Petroleum Company. " As before, Samuel got the House of Rothschild to finance the companies." (Z. 2, p. 23).

" Standard Oil's first desperate onslaught upon Royal Dutch was discontinued only when the Americans realised that Rothschild's millions were behind the Dutch company." (Z. 1, p. 53).

The Rothschilds were always hostile to the Tsars of Russia who were the only European monarchs to protect their people from the Jews by refusing to give them the status of Russians in Russia. They must, therefore, like Jacob Schiff of Kuhn Loeb & Co., have been interested in the success of Kerensky's revolution ; but it is impossible that the Rothschilds could have desired the success of the Bolshevik revolution which came next, because of the losses they would, and did, sustain in the Russian Oil-fields which were ultimately confiscated by the Soviet Government.

In the hope of recovering these oil-fields, the Rothschilds believing that the Bolsheviks would collapse, increased their holdings of Russian Oil-fields by further purchases made through Deterding, buying them at knock-down figures. We may be sure that they supported the counter-revolutionary attempts of Generals Wrangel, Deniken, and Admiral Kolchak, which all failed. It is interesting to note that the Brigadier-General of the British Military Mission to aid Denikin (1919-1920) and the Commanding Officer of the British Mission with Wrangel's forces (1920) was Sir J. Percy whose real name is Baumgartner and married to a Jewess, and the British High Commissioner in South Russia (1919-20) was Sir H. J. Mackinder, ex-Director of the London School of Economics, and also married to a Jewess ! Deterding himself married the daughter of a Russian " White " General.

The Royal Dutch Company which so strongly represents the Rothschilds also controls the Anglo-Saxon Petroleum Company, which has two peculiarities :—

> 1. It hardly ever is able to find Oil in British territories, although its concessions range all over the Empire's Crown Colonies, besides South Africa, Egypt and Palestine.

2. There is little that is Anglo-Saxon in the composition of its Directorate. It is strongly Jewish, and is part owner of the Consolidated Petroleum Co. and the Anglo-Mexican Petroleum Co. which in turn controls the Shell-Mex Companies of Argentine, Chile and Uruguay.

The number of books written about "Oil-wars" is Legion; and it will be noted that in all the international crises caused by conflicting interests chiefly between American Standard Oil and the European Royal Dutch, the Rothschilds have held strong position in the latter Company.

Under the Rothschild Paris regime, France found that she had neglected her Colonial oil-fields and suffered for it in the Great War 1914-18. Why was this allowed? R. Neumann blandly explains in his book *Zaharoff: the Armaments King* (1935), p. 210 :—"It was known that it was in the interests of the foreign oil trust that France should not discover any oil-wells in her own soil or in any of her colonial territories, for then she would remain permanently under the control of the foreign oil producers."

And there you have also the explanation of the curious non-discovery of Oil in British territories. It is, however, so necessary for the Jews to have Hitlerism destroyed, that we should not be surprised to hear of many wonderful new discoveries of Oil in British and French possessions, although such discoveries must not be expected until the highest prices have been wrung out of the taxpayers of both countries for the benefit of the oil-fields already working.

Among the major Oil-Wars we note the following theatres :—

1. *Mexico.* Here the game was the corruption of successive Presidents by the two belligerents (Standard Oil and Deterding), or, where that did not work, they resorted to the financing of revolutions against such Presidents or the forcing of "incidents" rendering "necessary" the landing of armed forces. One side was just as bad as the other, and thus they made of Mexico a shuttlecock, caring nothing for the welfare of the Mexican people and rendering good government there an impossibility.

2. *Venezuela.* The Oil-war in this country consisted chiefly in a duel of bribery of President Gomez from 1928 onward, the belligerents being Standard Oil and Deterding. This oil-war completely prevented good government in Venezuela, and made it possible for Gomez to reign as a most barbarous dictator to the intense suffering of the Venezuelan people.

3. *Asia Minor.* The Turko-Greek war (1920) in this country was really an oil-war, Greece being backed by "Britain" and Turkey by "France." When Turkey won, we sent her an ultimatum to yield to us the Oil-field, but then the U.S.A. stepped in and obtained a concession for oil which made Turkey her ally! Britain's reply to that situation was to begin to jib at paying her War-debts to the U.S.A. and that brought the U.S.A. to heel. The dispute was referred to the League of Nations, and Iraq gained the oil-field under a 25 years' British Mandate.

CHAPTER XIV.

DIAMONDS AND GOLD.

IT is said that when Lord Randolph Churchill made his extensive tour through South Africa in 1891 he was acting as agent to obtain information for the Rothschilds, who, of course, knew of the diamonds and gold which were being worked there. He took with him on these travels a mining engineer and does not seem to have himself followed up the favourable reports that this professional made to him. It would seem unnatural for a Churchill to perform work which was not in aid of some Jewish interest.

However that may be, it was 3 years before this when Cecil Rhodes applied to the London Rothschilds to buy out the French interests in the Kimberley mines and so obtain control of the Diamond industry in South Africa. For this purpose, Rhodes was financed by the Rothschilds to the extent of £1,400,000, and soon afterwards (with Barnato, to whom £5,338,000 was paid), the De Beers Consolidated Mines was formed, and the Rothschilds put in the Jew Sir Carl Meyer as their watchdog director. Out of the first deal, Rothschilds made £100,000 in 3 months by the rise in value of the Company's shares; they got a further £100,000 commission for the purchase of the De Beers mine. The Chairman of the De Beers Consolidated Mines is now the Jew Sir Ernest Oppenheimer. Sir Alfred Beit (Jew) is a Life Governor. The Diamond mining industry is a complete monopoly, and the price of these beautiful stones is kept up by artificial means so that no-one but the rich may acquire them, and the enormous profits pour into the hands of the Jews.

Before that, the Rothschilds " had long been interested behind the scenes, together with the Mosenthals, in London and South African Exploration Co." (L., p. 107). They took a financial interest also in the enormously powerful firm of Wernher Beit and Co., which owned huge tracts of land and gold mines in South Africa. " When Beit realised that it would be necessary to obtain the support of international financiers and bankers in order to raise all the capital required for the gold-mining industry, he decided to broaden the market by giving participations to the Rothschilds of Germany, Austria and France." So writes J. B. Taylor, of Wernher Beit & Co. in his *A Pioneer looks back*, 1939, p. 109.

To this day, the De Beers Company dominates the South African Press. According to the *Daily Telegraph*, 8th January, 1935, it was at Tring Park, the residence of Baron Nathaniel Rothschild, that Rhodes met the leading politicians of Britain. It is well known that the South African War was brought about by the Jews to obtain a strangle-hold on South African gold by means of the Union Jack, which they were unable to do under the rule of the crafty old Boer President Kruger. According to *Randlords*, by P. H. Emden (1935), it was the Rothschilds who backed financially the offer made to Portugal to purchase Delagoa Bay with the object of encircling the Transvaal of the Boers, the sum offered being £700,000.

Most significant of all is the information given by Dr. Hans Sauer in his book *From Africa*, 1937; Dr. Sauer was present in Westminster

Hall when the Parliamentary Committee was examining Rhodes on his part in the Jameson raid which fomented the outbreak of the war, and says he noticed " that the evidence was taken in a curious way and always went to ground like a hard-pressed fox whenever it began to point too strongly at certain persons." Sauer asked Rhodes the reason for this ; Rhodes replied " One of the big men knew all about it."

In discussing Sauer's book, the *Cape Times*, 2nd Nov., 1937, identifies the " big man " as (the late) Lord Rosebery ! Rhodes told Sauer that he had discussed the possibility of the raid with Lord Rosebery when the latter was Prime Minister ! The dates of Rosebery's Ministry were 1894-5, at which time he was a widower, his wife having been a Rothschild, and his children half-caste Rothschilds !

Now as Lord Rosebery and his Jewish friends and relations evidently arranged the Jameson Raid, the reader may guess what they must all have " made " by " bearing " the mining shares on the Johannesburg Bourse.

In the jargon of the stock exchange, a " bear " is one who sells shares, which he does not actually possess, for future delivery with a view to a drop in prices meanwhile ; when that drop in values occurs, he buys the shares and delivers them to his customer. The weapon of the successful " bear " is thus seen to be possession of information on coming events.

These Jews knew what was coming, for they arranged it to happen ; the Jameson Raid (1895) produced a fearful slump, and the Jews made millions as " bears."

Four " leaders " of the raid, including the Jew Lionel Phillips, were sentenced to death by a British Court, but the black cap meant nothing where Rothschilds were concerned, so the prisoners were able to buy their lives by a fine of £25,000 per head ! Soon after this, there was a perfect epidemic of Jewish baronetcies among those intimately concerned with the dastardly business of the Raid. Cecil Rhodes was rewarded by becoming a Director of De Beers in 1900.

The Jameson Raid provoked the costly (in life and treasure) South African War, 1899-1902. Speeches made by President Kruger in 1899 prove that he knew that the Jews, not the British, were his real enemies. " If it were conceivable," he said, speaking in Johannesburg market-place, in February, " to eject the Jew monopolist from this country neck and crop without incurring war with Great Britain, then the problem of everlasting peace would be solved."

Not only do the Rothschilds control the mining of South African gold, but they control also its price. In London, all gold bullion passes through the hands of three Jewish firms who govern the price of gold from day to day ; these are N. M. Rothschild & Sons, Mocatta & Goldsmid, and Samuel Montagu & Co.

CHAPTER XV.

ROTHSCHILDS AND ZIONISM.

IN general it may be said that until recently the Rothschild family has opposed Zionism on the grounds that it would be dangerous for their status as "citizens" of the various nations they infested.

Mayer Amschel Rothschild, the son of the original Amschel Mayer, refused in 1845 to have anything to do with Zionism.

Edmond Rothschild also opposed political Zionism, although the Jewish colonies in Palestine before the war really owed their existence to his donations. In 1900 he ceded his eight "colonies" in Palestine to the Jewish Colonisation Association. But he approached Lord Bertie of Thame about a National Home in Palestine on 25th January, 1915. (P, p. 105).

Nathaniel in England was also an opponent of Zionism, until he met Theodor Herzl, the Zionist leader, in 1902, when, alone in the Rothschild family he endorsed the project for making a National Home for the Jews in East Africa.

After a while, the resistance of other Rothschilds to Zionist ideas was worn down, and Balfour made his notorious " Declaration " of 1917 as an address to Baron Lionel Walter Rothschild.

The first Zionist political committee's meeting on 7th Feb., 1917, had been attended by Lionel Walter and by James Rothschild, son of Edmond.

CHAPTER XVI.

OTHER ROTHSCHILDS.

CERTAIN Jewish families named Rothschild, apparently unconnected by blood with the family with which this book chiefly deals, are prominent in America, and one, *Walter N. Rothschild* is the husband of Carola Warburg, granddaughter of Jacob Schiff, the founder of the New York Jewish bankers Kuhn Loeb & Co., who, after the Great War, 1914-1918, were backing Jew-run Republican Germany with a view to control of politics there, whilst the European Rothschilds in London and Paris were favouring France.

But the most important of the mysterious Rothschilds is the Jew known to-day as " the French Disraeli," *George Mandel*, whom Alfred Rosenberg (the Nazi Minister) and French anti-Jewish workers state is really *Jeroboam Rothschild*. He certainly exhibits the symptoms of official Rothschild backing, for he appears to be indispensible to all Governments in France, whatever their labels may be, whilst his policy is always in accord with that of the Banque de France, which the Paris House of Rothschild always dominates by a member of it acting as Regent. Mandel is a member of the Jewish Masonic Order B'nai B'rih and of Grand Orient Masonry. During the Peace Conference at Versailles he was secretary to Clemenceau ; it will be remembered that Lloyd George had Sir Philip Sassoon as his secretary, and that Sir

Philip's mother was a Rothschild; which is just what might have been expected.

Mandel was also Clemenceau's secretary during the War itself.

Since the war, he has been the principal advocate in France of an alliance with Bolshevik Russia, and worked against an understanding with Fascist Italy. He controls *L'Ami du Peuple.*

Hon. E. M. Stonor, a brother of Baron Camoys, married as his second wife the daughter of *Thos. Wm. Rothschild* of Pretoria in 1925 but there was no issue of the marriage·

CHAPTER XVII.

THE MORAL OF IT ALL.

THERE is a very definite moral to this narrative of events. It is this:—Only a minority of men and women in any community, of any race and of any rank, and of any religion, are strong enough to withstand absolutely the influence exercised upon them by those who wield Money Power, which becomes without much effort the real ruler of " democratic " governments, When that Money Power is wielded by Jews, it follows that democracy is condemned by its very nature to result in the rule by alien Jews of the country which adopts it.

It is not to be supposed that all those who have done the Rothschilds' Jewish work for them in international politics have been bribed. Many of them, like Prince Metternich or Lord Kitchener, were men of high personal honour, to whom it would be unthinkable that even a Jew would dare to offer a bribe.

The influence of money is generally exerted in a far more subtle manner than that of raw bribery. Even good men and women, if they are not also strong, find it difficult to resist favours such as presents given under circumstances which make refusal difficult or churlish; " tips " as to the likely future fluctuations in value of stocks and shares; introductions to influential people afforded by the rich to the needy; residential accommodation supplied at a cost considerably below that which is usual for such accommodation; the supply of early news to politicians; and so forth and so on. Under such influences, people who could not be bribed by any direct means, find themselves placed sooner or later in circumstances where it is impossible for them to refuse some sort of return of the favours, a return which perhaps the official position of the individual concerned affords him the opportunity to make. That is the thin edge of the wedge. The Jew craftily taps the wedge further home, driving it as far as he dares, and in some cases probably completing control over his prey by resounding hammer blows upon that wedge until personality and honour begin to part company.

Democracy, the great political fraud, must be scrapped and the nation and the empire must be placed in the hands of a few great patriots whose race and character are above suspicion, and under whose influence even fallen Royalty can regain its sense of serious duty.

INDEX.

www.ingramcontent.com/pod-product-compliance
Lightning Source LLC
Chambersburg PA
CBHW052106270326
41931CB00012B/2901